QUILTED ADVENTURES

BY SARA NEPHEW

CONTENTS

DEDICATION

To Artists everywhere, quilter or painter, child or adult. You really know how to have fun!

ACKNOWLEDGEMENTS

Heartfelt thanks to the adventurous quilters who helped test my patterns and piece samples for this book: Anette Austin, Laurie Bevan, Dianne Coombs, Joan Dawson, Eda Lee Haas, Scott Hansen, Roxi Lewis, Jean Look-Krischano, and Kathleen Springer. They are patient with the author when a book slows or a pattern changes. Their creativity adds luster to my quilt designs.

CREDITS

Photography by Terry Reed
Cover Graphics by Elizabeth Nephew

QUILTED ADVENTURES

Clearview Triangle
8311 180th St. S.E.
Snohomish, WA 98296-4802
Library of Congress Control Number: 2002096390
ISBN 1-930294-03-4

ADVENTURE BLOCKS

FREIGHT CAR

1½" finished square
5" x 9½" block with seam allowance

Cut for one block:

1.	2 freight car	3½"	square
2.	1 background	2" x 3½"	rectangle
3.	1 door, 1 bckgrnd	2" x 2¾"	rectangle
4.	2 wheel, 2 bkgrnd	2"	square
5.	1 freight car, 1 wheel	1¼" x 2"	rectangle

Piecing Diagram

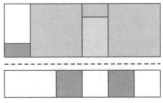

Directions:

1. Assemble according to the piecing diagram.

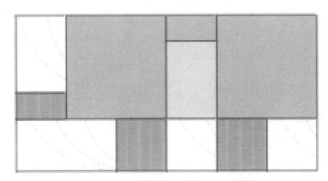

3

TRUCK

Cut for one block:

1.	1 truck	5" x 8"	rectangle
2.	1 truck	2¾" x 3½"	rectangle
3.	1 background	2" x 6½"	rectangle
4.	1 background	2" x 3½"	rectangle
5.	1 truck	2" x 2¾"	rectangle
6.	4 tire, 1 window, 5 bkgrnd	2"	square
7.	1 background	1¼" x 3½"	rectangle
8.	1 background	1¼" x 2"	rectangle

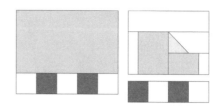

Piecing Diagram

Directions:

1. Place a window 2" square on one end of a background 2" x 3½" rectangle and sew a diagonal seam as shown. Outside the stitching, trim fabric to a ¼" seam. Press to the dark. Assemble according to the piecing diagram.

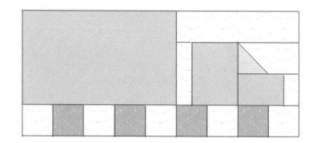

JET

Cut for one block:

1.	1 jet	2" x 9½"	rectangle
2.	2 jet, 4 sky	2" x 3½"	rectangle
3.	1 jet, 5 sky	2"	square

Directions:

1. Make these pieces:

A. Place a jet 2" square on one end of a sky 2" x 3½" rectangle and sew a diagonal seam as shown. Outside the stitching, trim fabric to a ¼" seam. Press to the dark.

B. Place a sky 2" square on one end of a jet 2" x 3½" rectangle and sew a diagonal seam. Trim and press. Place a sky 2" square on the other end. Sew the same diagonal, trim and press. Make another one of these, but sew to the opposite diagonals.

C. Place a sky 2" square on one end of a jet 2" x 9½" rectangle and sew a diagonal seam as shown. Trim and press to the dark.

2. Assemble according to the piecing diagram.

A.

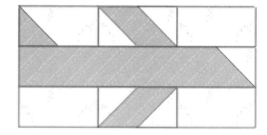

B.

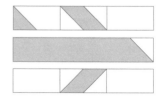

Piecing Diagram

C.

SCHOOL BUS

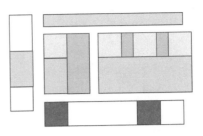

1½" finished square
6½" x 11" block with seam allowance

Cut for one block:

1.	1 bus	2¾" x 6½"	rectangle
2.	1 background	2" x 5"	rectangle
3.	1 door	2" x 4¼"	rectangle
4.	2 bus, 1 bckgrnd	2" x 2¾"	rectangle
5.	1 window	2" x 4"	strip
6.	2 window, 2 tire	2"	square
7.	2 background	2"	square
8.	1 bus	1¼" x 9½"	rectangle
9.	1 door	1¼" x 4"	strip

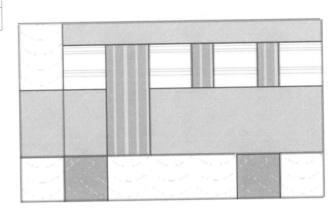

Piecing Diagram

Directions:

1. Sew the door 1¼" x 4" strip and the window 2" x 4" strip together lengthwise. Cut two 2" sections from this set of strips.

2. Assemble according to the piecing diagram.

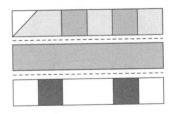

BIG VAN

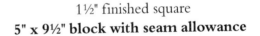

1½" finished square
5" x 9½" block with seam allowance

Cut for one block:

1.	1 van	2" x 9½	rectangle
2.	1 window	2" x 3½"	rectangle
3.	1 background	2" x 3½"	rectangle
4.	3 bckgrnd, 2 van	2"	square
5.	2 wheel, 2 window	2"	square

Piecing Diagram

Directions:

1. Place a background 2" square on one end of a van 2" x 3½" rectangle and sew a diagonal seam as shown. Outside the stitching, trim fabric to a ¼" seam. Press to the triangle.

2. Assemble according to the piecing diagram.

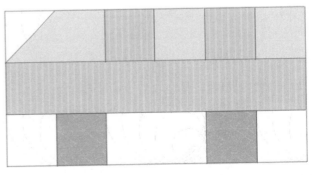

5

HELICOPTER

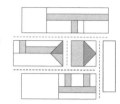

1½" finished square
9½" x 11" block with seam allowance

Cut for one block:

1.	1 sky	3½" x 5"	rectangle
2.	1 sky	3½"	square
3.	2 sky	2" x 6½"	rectangle
4.	1 copter, 1 window, 2 sky	2" x 3½"	rectangle
5.	1 copter, 1 window, 3 sky	2"	square
6.	1 copter, 1 sky	1¼" x 27"	strip

Piecing Diagram

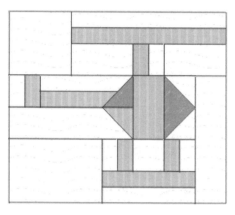

Directions:

1. Sew the 1¼" helicopter and sky strips together lengthwise. Cut from this set of strips:

A.	one	8"	section
B.	two	5"	section
C.	four	2"	section

2. (A)Place a window 2" square on one end of a 5" strip section from above. Sew a diagonal seam as shown. Outside the stitching, trim fabric to ¼" seam. Press to the triangle. (B) Place a helicopter 2" square on one end of a sky 2" x 6½" rectangle. Sew to the opposite diagonal. Trim and press.

A.

B.

3.

3. Sew two sky 2" squares diagonally on the ends of the 2" x 3 ½" window rectangle with a diagonal seam and its opposite as shown. Trim and press to the triangles. Assemble according to the piecing diagram.

LITTLE VAN

1½" finished square
5" x 8" block with seam allowance

Reverse

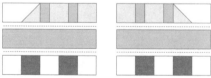

Piecing Diagram

Cut for one block:

1.	1 van	2" x 8"	rectangle
2.	1 background	2" x 3½"	rectangle
3.	3 window, 2 wheel	2"	square
4.	3 background	2"	square
5.	2 van	1¼" x 2"	rectangle

Directions:

1. Place a window 2" square on one end of the background 2" x 3½" rectangle and sew a corner to corner diagonal seam as shown. To make a reverse van, reverse this piece.) Outside the stitching, trim fabric to a ¼" seam. Press to the dark. Assemble according to the piecing diagram.

Reverse

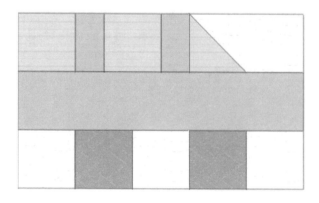

PICKUP

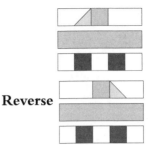
Piecing Diagram

Reverse

Cut for one block:

1.	1 truck and 1 background	2" x 8"	rectangle
2.	2 background	2" x 3½"	rectangle
3.	1 window, 2 tire, 1 truck, 3 bkgrnd	2"	square

Directions:

1. Place a window 2" square on one end of a background 2" x 3½" rectangle and sew a diagonal seam as shown. (For a reverse truck, reverse this piece.) Outside the stitching, trim fabric to a ¼" seam. Press to the dark.

Reverse

2. Assemble according to the piecing diagram.

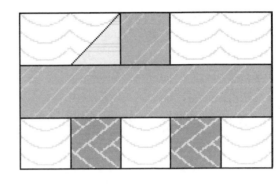

SEDAN

Cut for one block:

1.	1 car and 1 background	2" x 9½"	rectangle
2.	3 background	2" x 3½"	rectangle
3.	2 tire, 3 window, 2 bkgrnd	2"	square
4.	2 car	¼" x 2"	rectangle

Piecing Diagram

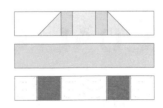

Directions:

1. Place a window 2" square on one end of a background 2" x 3½" rectangle and sew a diagonal seam as shown. Outside the stitching, trim fabric to a ¼" seam. Press to the triangle. Make another one of these sewn to the opposite diagonal.

2. Assemble according to the piecing diagram.

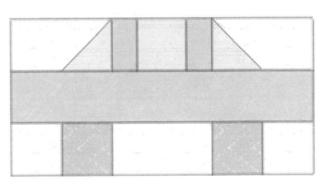

LOCOMOTIVE

Cut for one block: (Cut and assemble the cowcatcher#1 first, then cut pieces from the leftover triangles.)

1.	1 cowcatcher, 1 background	3⅞"	square
2.	1 locomotive	2¾" x 8"	rectangle
3.	1 background	2¾"	square
4.	2 bckgrnd, 5 locomotive	2"	square
5.	1 background	1¼" x 8¾"	rectangle
6.	1 locomotive	1¼" x 2¾"	rectangle
7.	3 background, 1 locomotive	1¼" x 2"	rectangle
8.	2 background, 1 locomotive	1¼"	square

Piecing Diagram

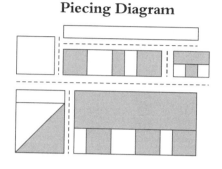

Directions:

1. Cut the background and cowcatcher 3⅞" squares in half diagonally. Sew one of each of the resulting triangles together to make a large half-square. You will have one of each triangle left over to cut smaller pieces from.

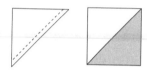

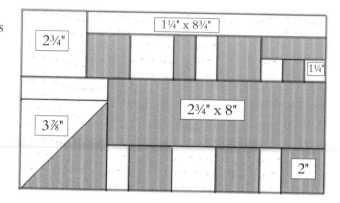

2. Assemble according to the piecing diagram.

COAL CAR

Cut for one block:

1.	1 coal car	3½" x 5"	rectangle
2.	1 background	2" x 2¾"	rectangle
3.	3 bckgrnd, 2 wheel	2"	square
4.	1 background	1¾" x 2"	rectangle

Piecing Diagram

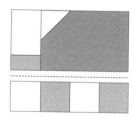

Directions:

1. Place a background 2" square on the upper left corner of the coal car 3½" x 5" rectangle and sew a corner to corner diagonal seam as shown. Outside the stitching, trim fabric to a ¼" seam. Press to the dark.

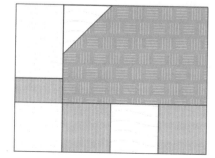

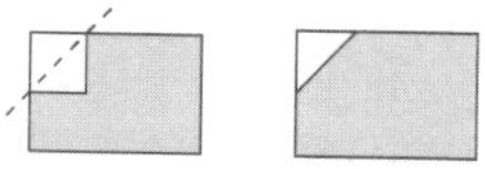

2. Assemble according to the piecing diagram.

COACH CAR

Cut for one block:

1.	1 door, 1 bckgrnd	2" x 2¾"	rectangle
2.	2 wheel, 3 bckgrnd	2"	square
3.	1 coach car, 1 bckgrnd	1¼" x 11"	strip
4.	1 coach car	1¼" x 8"	rectangle
5.	2 coach car	1¼" x 3½"	rectangle
6.	1 wheel	1¼" x 2"	rectangle

Piecing Diagram

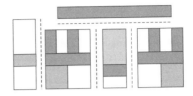

Directions:

1. Sew the 1¼" x 11" strips together lengthwise. Cut five 2" sections from this set of strips.

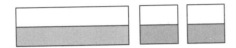

2. Assemble according to the piecing diagram.

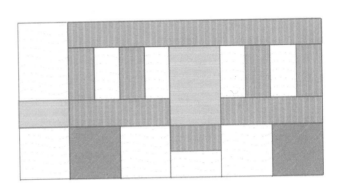

CABOOSE

Cut for one block:

1.	1 door, 2 caboose	2" x 2¾"	rectangle
2.	2 background	2" x 2¾"	rectangle
3.	2 wheel, 1 background	2"	square
4.	1 roof	1¼" x 6½"	rectangle
5.	1 bckgrnd, 1 wheel	1¼" x 2"	strip
6.	1 caboose, 2 window	1¼" x 3"	strip

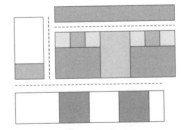

Piecing Diagram

Directions:

1. Sew the 1¼" x 3" window and caboose strips together lengthwise as shown. Cut two 1¼" sections from this set of strips.

Waste ➡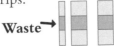

2. Assemble according to the piecing diagram.

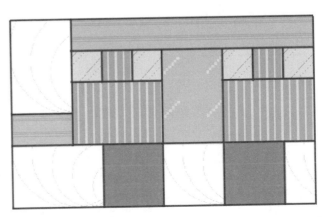

BICYCLIST

		1½" finished square 12½" block with seam allowance

Cut for one block:

1.	1 shirt and 1 background	3⅞"	square
2.	1 background	3½" x 6½"	rectangle
3.	1 road	2" x 12½"	rectangle
4.	1 pants and 1 background	2" x 5"	rectangle
5.	1 pants and 2 background	2" x 3½"	rectangle
6.	1 bike and 1 background	1¼" x 21"	strip
7.	1 shirt and 1 background	1¼" x 6"	strip
8.	1 foot, 1 face, 8 bike, 17 bkgrnd	2"	square
9.	1 background	1¼"	square

Directions:

1. Cut the background and shirt 3⅞" squares in half diagonally. Sew one of each of the resulting triangles together as shown to make a large half-square. (You will have one of each left for another block.) *(Note: If you are making the* Riding Bikes *quilt, you may wish to use one of the speed methods described on pg.11.)* Place a background 1¼" square on the shirt corner of this large half-square and sew a diagonal seam as shown.

2. Sew the 1¼" bike and background strips together lengthwise. Cut from this set of strips:

1	3½" section
11	2" section

Sew the 1¼" x 6" shirt and background strips together lengthwise. Cut from this set of strips:

1	3½" section
1	2" section

3. Place a background 2" square on one end of a 2" x 3½" pants rectangle and sew a diagonal seam as shown. Outside the stitching, trim fabric to a ¼" seam. Press to the triangle. Place another background 2" square on the other end and sew the same diagonal. Trim and press.

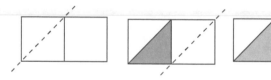

4. Place a foot and a background 2" square right sides together and sew a corner to corner diagonal seam. Trim on one side to a quarter inch seam allowance. Press to the dark. This is a 2" half-square. Make one face-hair half-square. Make eight bike-background half-squares. *(Note: If you are making the* Riding Bikes *quilt, you may wish to use your favorite speed method to produce 2" half-squares in quantity.)*

5. Assemble according to the piecing diagram.

Tip: *Use paper pieced half-squares, bias squares, iron-on guide lines, or: On the back of your light fabric, carefully draw a grid of squares (2⅜" for 2" half-squares, 3⅞" for 3½" half-squares). Draw diagonal lines in one direction through the corners of the squares. Place right sides together with a piece of dark fabric. Sew seams ¼" away on both sides of the diagonal lines. Then cut on all drawn lines to produce many half-squares. Press open. (The drawing at right would make 50 half-squares.)*

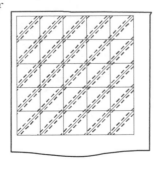

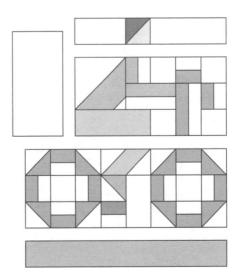

Piecing Diagram

HOT-AIR BALLOON

Cut for one block: (omit #1 if doing Seminole piecing below)

1.	1 balloon	3½" x 6½"	rectangle
2.	1 balloon, 1 sky	3⅛"	square
3.	1 balloon	2" x 6½"	rectangle
4.	1 balloon	2" x 2¾"	rectangle
5.	2 sky	2¾"	square
6.	1 basket and 2 sky	2"	square
7.	1 sky	1¼" x 2"	rectangle

Directions:

1. Place the sky and balloon 3⅛" squares right sides together. Draw a diagonal line on the back of the lightest fabric. Stitch ¼" away from the line on both sides. Cut on the drawn line to produce two large half-squares.

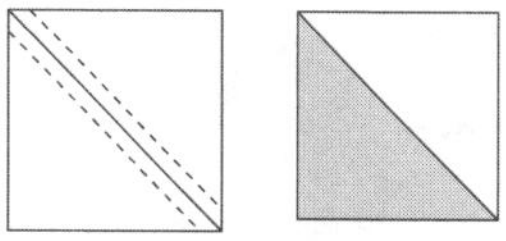

2. Place a sky 2" square on one end of the balloon 2" x 6½" rectangle and sew a diagonal seam as shown. Outside the stitching, trim fabric to a ¼" seam. Press to the triangle. Sew another sky 2" square on the other end as shown. Trim and press.

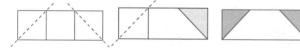

3. If desired, instead of the 3½" x 6½" balloon rectangle, make a panel of Seminole piecing according to one of the plans at right for the body of the balloon.

4. **Ropes:** Draw light pencil lines ⅜" from left and right short edge of the 1¼" x 2" sky rectangle. Sew a ⅝" x 1¼" bias strip of rope fabric on each pencil line with a ¼" seam as shown. (Edge of the rope fabric will be ⅛" from the short edges of the sky rectangle.) Then press rope fabric back over the stitching as shown.

Assemble according to the piecing diagram. *Or: After assembling the block, embroider ropes on the vertical seams between the basket and the balloon.*

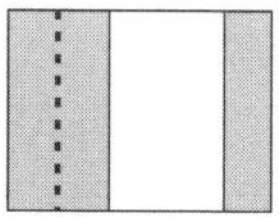

Seminole Piecing

Cut and sew according to one of the charts below: You may be able to get three balloons from each 40" strip set.

A. Four different 1¼" strips
Sew lengthwise
Cut 1¼" strip sections
Move squares from top to bottom of each strip in order, to create the pattern (Eight strips will complete one 6½" unit shown in block diagram.)
Sew strips together in order, butting seams, to make 3½" x 6½" pieced unit

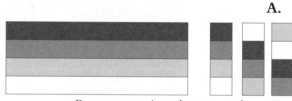
A.

Resew squares in each row to make pattern

B. Five different 1¼" strips
Sew lengthwise, offsetting each strip one inch
Cut 3½" sections at 45° angle
Connect and trim to make 3½" x 6½" pieced unit

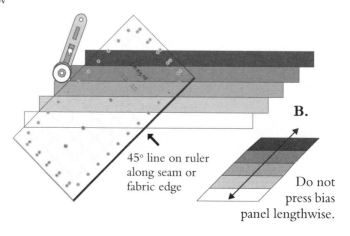

45° line on ruler along seam or fabric edge

B.

Do not press bias panel lengthwise.

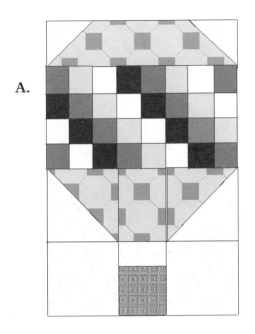

A.

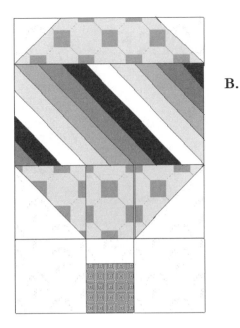

B.

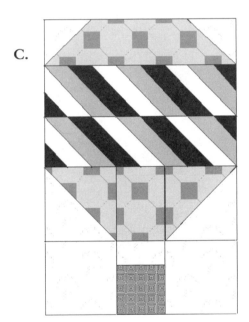

C.

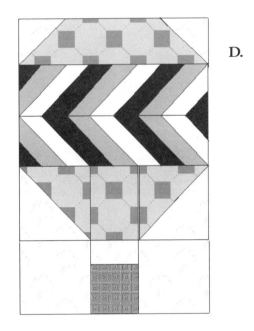

D.

C. Three different 1¼" strips
Sew lengthwise, then cut 2" sections at 45° angle
Connect and trim to make 6½" panel
Make another panel, but remove strip from end
and add to beginning to offset colors by one position
Sew together and trim panels to make 3½" x 6½"
pieced unit

C.

seam 45° sections,
offset colors in
second strip,
trim & join

D. Three different 1¼" strips
Sew lengthwise
Fold over and cut 2" sections at 45° angle
Connect and trim to make 6½" panel (use three sets)
Make another panel at reverse angle, same color order
Sew together and trim panels to make 3½" x 6½" unit

D.

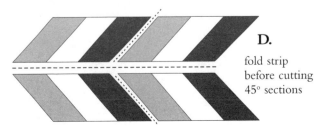

fold strip
before cutting
45° sections

TOPPLANE

Cut for one block:

1.	2 sky	6½" x 8"	rectangle
2.	2 plane	3½" x 8"	rectangle
3.	2 sky	3½" x 6½"	rectangle
4.	2 sky, 1 plane	2" x 6½"	rectangle
5.	2 sky	2" x 5"	rectangle
6.	3 plane, 1 cockpit	2" x 3½"	rectangle
7.	10 sky, 2 plane	2"	square
8.	1 sky, 1 plane	1¼" x 14"	strip
9.	1 sky, 1 prop	1¼" x 6½"	strip
10.	2 plane	1¼" x 3½"	rectangle

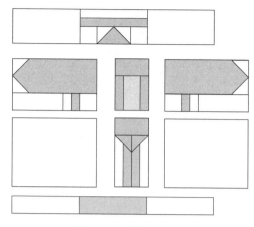

Piecing Diagram

Directions:

1. Sew the plane and sky 1¼" x 14"strips together lengthwise. Cut sections below from this set of strips.

two	5" section
two	2" section

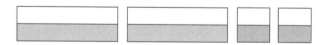

2. Place a plane 2" square on the right end of a 5" strip section from #1 above and sew a diagonal seam as shown. Outside the stitching, trim fabric to a ¼" seam. Press to the square. Make another of these, but reversed as shown.

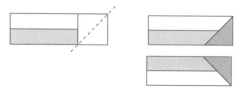

3. Sew a sky 2" square diagonally on one corner of a 3½" x 8" plane rectangle as shown. Trim and press to the square. Sew another sky 2" square on the adjacent corner as shown. Trim and press. Make two of these.

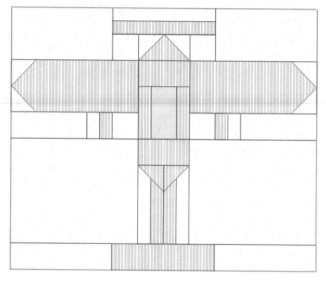

4. Place a sky 2" square on one end of a plane 2" x 3½" rectangle and sew a diagonal seam as shown. Outside the stitching, trim fabric to a ¼" seam. Press to the square. Place a sky 2" square on the other end. Sew the opposite diagonal, trim and press.

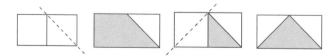

5. Assemble according to the piecing diagram.

SIDEPLANE

Cut for one block:

1.	1 sky	3½" x 5"	rectangle
2.	4 sky	2" x 5"	rectangle
3.	3 plane	2" x 3½"	rectangle
4.	8 sky, 1 tire	2"	square
5.	1 sky, 1 plane	1¼" x 10"	strip
6.	1 plane	1¼" x 6½"	rectangle
7.	1 plane, wing, sky	1¼" x 5"	strip
8.	1 wing, prop, sky	1¼" x 3½"	strip
9.	1 plane	1¼" x 2"	rectangle
10.	4 sky	1"	square

Piecing Diagram

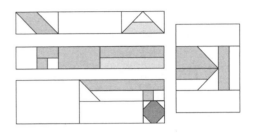

Directions:

1. Sew the plane and sky 1¼" x 10" strips together lengthwise. Cut sections from this set of strips:

one	3½" section
one	1¼" section

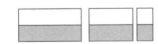

2. A. Sew one 1¼" section from #1 above onto the end of the 1¼" x 5" sky strip as shown. B. Sew the plane 1¼" x 6½" rectangle onto (A) lengthwise as shown. Place a sky 2" square on the left end of (B) and sew a diagonal seam as shown. Outside the stitching, trim fabric to a ¼" seam. Press to the square. C. Place a sky 2" square on the right end of a 3½" plane-sky strip section and sew a diagonal seam as shown. Trim and press to the square.

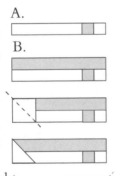

3. Sew a sky 2" square on one end of the 2" x 3½" plane rectangle with a diagonal seam as shown. Trim and press to the dark. Make two of these. Take one and sew a sky 2" square on the other end with the same diagonal as shown. Trim and press.

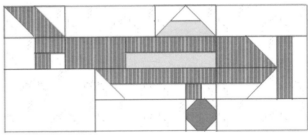

4. Sew the wing and sky 1¼" x 3½" strips together lengthwise. Place a 2" sky square on one end of this sky-wing strip set and sew diagonally as shown. Trim and press to the square. Place a sky 2" square on the other end and sew to the opposite diagonal. Trim and press.

5. Place a sky 1" square on one corner of the tire 2" square and sew a diagonal seam as shown. Outside the stitching, trim fabric to a ¼" seam. Press to the square. Round all four corners in the same way.

6. Assemble according to the piecing diagram.

ANCHOR

Cut for one block:

1.	1 background, 1 anchor	3⅛"	square
2.	2 background	2" x 5"	rectangle
3.	2 background	2"	square
4.	2 background, 1 anchor	1¼" x 4¼"	rectangle
5.	4 background, 4 anchor	1¼" x 2¾"	rectangle
6.	2 anchor	1¼" x 2"	rectangle
7.	10 anchor, 7 background	1¼"	square

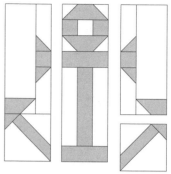

Piecing Diagram

Directions:

1. Place the background and anchor 3⅛" squares right sides together. Draw a diagonal line on the back of the lightest fabric. Stitch ¼" away from the line on both sides. Cut on the drawn line to produce two 2¾" half-squares.

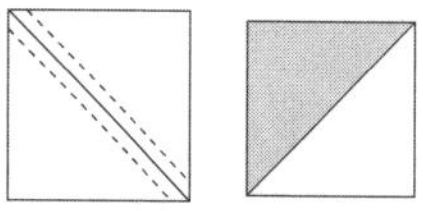

2. Place a 2" background square on the anchor corner of unit #1 above. Sew diagonally as shown. Trim and press to the 2" background square. Make two of these. Place an anchor 1¼" square on one of the anchor-background corners of this unit. Sew diagonally, trim, and press to the 1¼" square. Make one of these reversed.

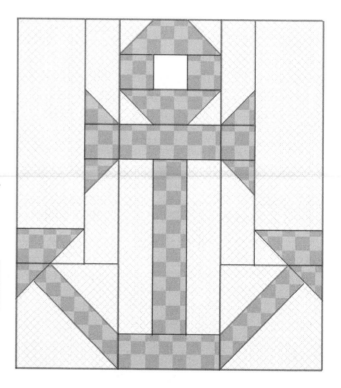

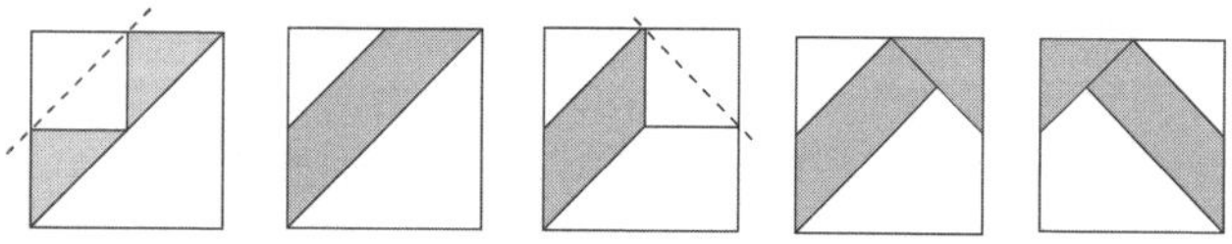

3. Make pieces according to the directions below:
A. Place a background 1¼" square on one end of an anchor 1¼" x 2" rectangle and sew a diagonal seam as shown. Outside the stitching, trim fabric to a ¼" seam. Press to the square. Make one of these reversed.

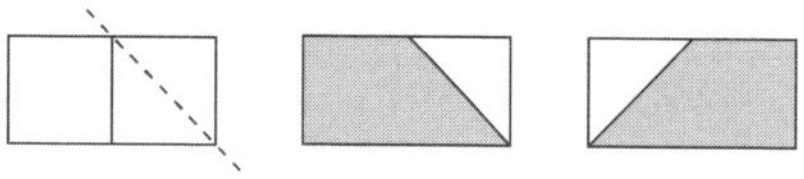

B. Place a anchor 1¼" square on one end of an background 1¼" x 2¾" rectangle and sew a diagonal seam as shown. Outside the stitching, trim fabric to a ¼" seam. Press to the square. Make two of these. Make two of these reversed.

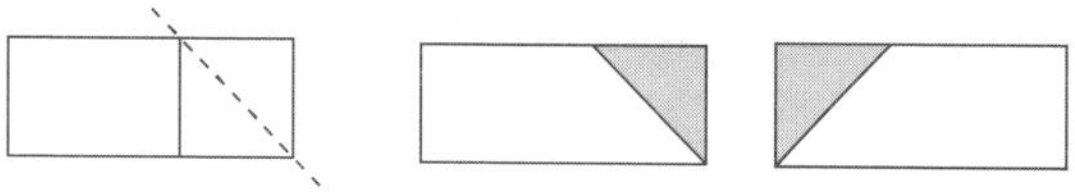

C. Place a background 1¼" square on one end of an anchor 1¼" x 2¾" rectangle and sew a diagonal seam as shown. Outside the stitching, trim fabric to a ¼" seam. Press to the square. Place a background 1¼" square on the other end and the opposite diagonal. Trim and press. Make two of these.

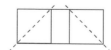

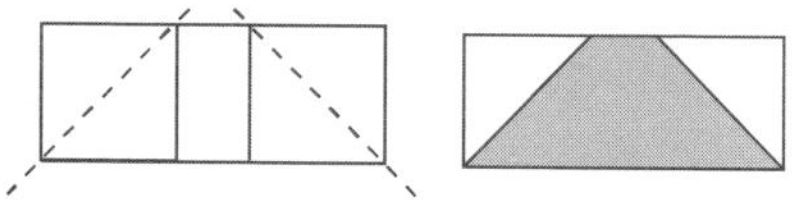

4. Assemble according to the piecing diagram.

SAILBOAT

Cut for one block:

1.	1 sail, 1 sky	3⅞"	square
2.	1 boat	2" x 5"	rectangle
3.	1 sky	2" x 3½"	rectangle
4.	1 sail, 2 water	2"	square

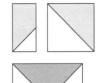

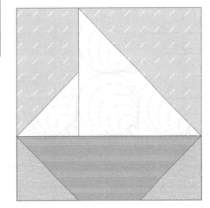

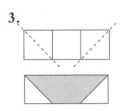

Piecing Diagram

3.

Directions:

1. Cut the sail and sky 3⅞" squares in half diagonally as shown. Sew one of each of the resulting triangles together to make a large half-square. You will have one of each left over for another block. *(Or use the speed method described in #1 on pg. 10.)*

2. Place a sail 2" square on one end of the sky 2" x 3½" rectangle and sew a diagonal seam as shown. Outside the stitching, trim fabric to a ¼" seam. Press to the triangle.

3. Sew a water 2" square on one corner of a boat 2" x 5" rectangle with a diagonal seam. Trim and press. Place a water 2" square on the other end of the rectangle. Sew the opposite diagonal. Assemble according to the piecing diagram.

SEAWEED

Directions:

1. Place a seaweed 2" square on the left end of a background 2" x 3½" rectangle and sew a diagonal seam as shown. Outside the stitching, trim fabric to a ¼" seam. Press to the triangle. Make as many of these basic units as needed for the length desired. Make reverse units for the other lengthwise half of the Seaweed Border.

2. Place a seaweed and background 2" square right sides together and sew a corner-to-corner diagonal seam. Trim one side to a quarter inch seam allowance. Press to the dark. This is a 2" half-square. Finish the end of the row with a half-square or a plain background square as needed.

3. Assemble in two vertical rows according to the piecing diagram. (As shown in the quilt.)

Basic Unit **Half Square**

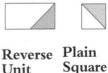

Reverse Unit **Plain Square**

This is a continuous border assembled in two vertical strips.

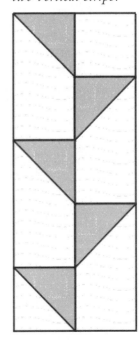

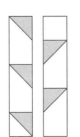

Piecing Diagram

TALL SHIP

Cut for one block:

1.	1 sail and 1 sky	8⅜"	square
2.	1 sail and 1 sky	6⅞"	square
3.	1 sky	6½"	square
4.	1 sail and 1 sky	5⅜"	square
5.	1 sail and 1 sky	3⅞"	square
6.	1 boat	3½" x 12½"	rectangle
7.	1 sky	3½" x 6½"	rectangle
8.	1 sail	3½" x 5"	rectangle
9.	1 water	2" x 18½"	rectangle
10.	2 sky	2" x 5"	rectangle
11.	1 sky	2" x 3½"	rectangle
12.	1 boat and 1 sky	1¼"x 6"	strip
13.	1 mast and 2 sky	1" x 16"	strip
14.	1 flag, 4 sky, 3 water, 2 boat	2"	square

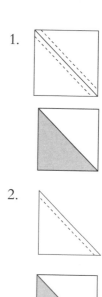

1.

2.

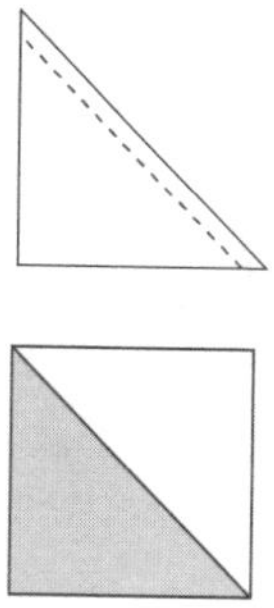

Directions:

1. Place the sky and sail 5⅜" squares right sides together. Draw a corner-to-corner diagonal line on the back of the lightest fabric. Stitch ¼" away from the line on both sides. Cut on the drawn line to produce two 5" half-squares. *(Note: If you are making the Tall Ships quilt, make the 8⅜", 6⅞", and 3⅞" half-squares using the above speed method. But if you are making just one block, you may wish to proceed as in #2 below.)*

2. Cut the sky and sail 8⅜", 6⅞", and 3⅞" squares in half diagonally as shown. Sew one of each of the resulting triangles together to make a large half-square. You will have one of each left for another block.

3. Make these pieces:
(A) Place a boat 2" square on one end of the sky 2" x 3½" rectangle and sew a diagonal seam as shown. Outside the stitching, trim fabric to a ¼" seam. Press to the triangle.
(B) Sew a flag 2" square on one end of a sky 2" x 5" rectangle with a diagonal seam as shown. Press to the triangle.

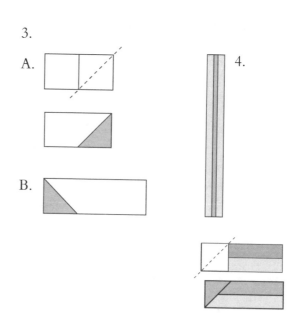

3.

A.

B.

4.

4. Sew the 1" x 16" mast and sky strips together lengthwise, with the mast strip in the middle. Cut the best 14" section from this set of strips. Sew the 1¼" x 6" boat and sky strips together lengthwise. Cut a 5" section from this set of strips. Place a boat 2" square on the left end of this strip section and sew a diagonal seam as shown.

TALL SHIP

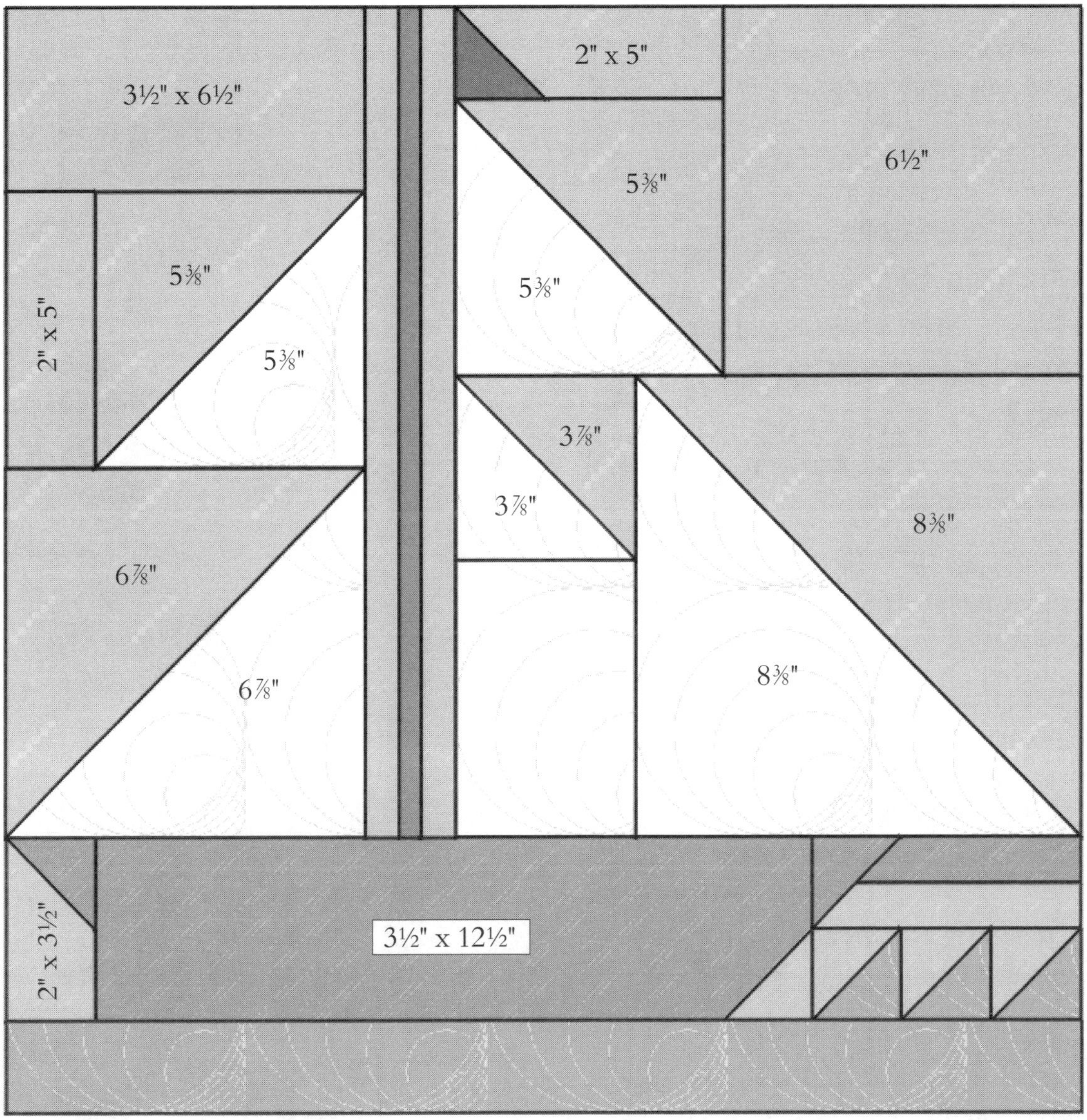

3½" x 6½"
2" x 5"
6½"
5⅜"
5⅜"
2" x 5"
5⅜"
5⅜"
3⅞"
3⅞"
8⅜"
6⅞"
6⅞"
8⅜"
2" x 3½"
3½" x 12½"

5. Sew a sky 2" square diagonally on the bottom right corner of the 3½" x 12½" boat rectangle with a diagonal seam as shown. Trim and press.

6. Place a water and a sky 2" square right sides together and sew a corner-to-corner diagonal seam. Trim on one side to a ¼" seam allowance. Press to the dark. This is a 2" half-square. Make three of these. Assemble according to the piecing diagram.

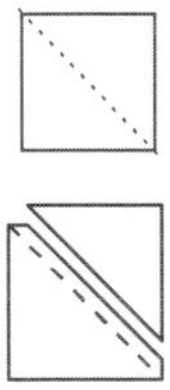

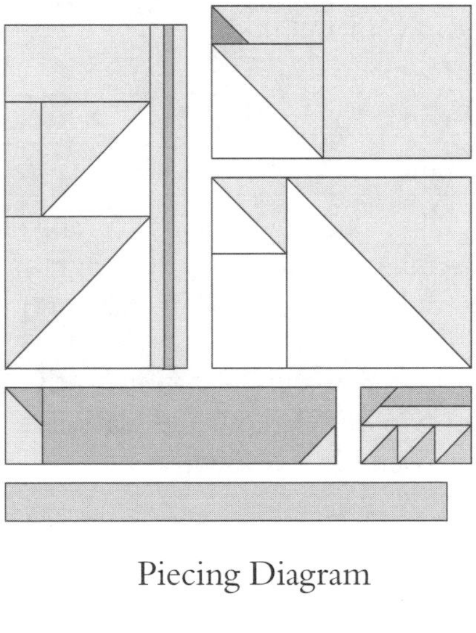

Piecing Diagram

NAUTICAL FLAGS

(Flag information is from ....
http://www.usps.org/f_stuff/signmean.html)
(Use the required colors, or if you don't care about the meaning of the flags, substitute any colors that please you.)

Directions: (from top to bottom on the quilt and at right)

"E" or "I am altering my course to starboard"
Cut a red and a blue 2" x 5" rectangle and sew the two together lengthwise as shown.

"T" or "Keep clear of me"
Cut a 2" x 3½" rectangle each of red, white, and blue and sew together as shown.

"D" or "Keep clear"
Cut two yellow 1¼" x 5" strips and one blue 2" x 5" strip and sew the yellow on either side of the blue.

"G" or "I require a pilot"
Cut one yellow and one blue 1¼" x 12" strip and sew them together lengthwise. Cut three 3½" sections from this strata. Sew together as shown.

"P" or "About to sail"
Cut for one flag:

1 white	2" x 2½"	rectangle
2 blue	1¾" x 2"	rectangle
2 blue	1¼" x 5"	strip

Sew the blue rectangles left and right of the white rectangle. Add the blue strips top and bottom.

"Stop your intention"
Cut for one flag:

4 white	1⅝" x 2⅜"	rectangle
2 blue	1¼" x 2⅜"	rectangle
1 blue	1¼" x 3½"	rectangle

Assemble according to the diagram. (Scott substituted different colors for this one.)

"L" or "You should stop instantly"
Cut two each yellow and black 2" x 2¾" rectangles and assemble as shown.

1½" finished square
Each flag is a 3½" x 5" block with seam allowance

"E"

"T"

"D"

"G"

"P"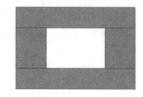

"Stop Your Intention"

"L"

SUN

Cut for one block:

1.	2 sky, 2 sun	3⅞"	square
2.	4 sky	2⅝	square
3.	1 sun	2" x 5"	rectangle
4.	2 sky, 1 sun	1" x 9"	strip
5.	6 sun	2"	square

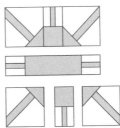

Piecing Diagram

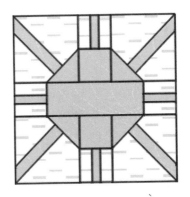

Directions:

1. A. Place the sky and sun 3⅞" squares right sides together. Draw a corner to corner diagonal line on the back of the lightest fabric. Stitch ¼" away from the line on both sides. Cut on the drawn line to produce two 3½" half-squares. Make two more of these.

A.

B.

B. Draw a corner-to-corner diagonal line on the back of the sky 2⅝" squares. Place one of these on the sun corner of the 3½" half-square from #1 above, with the diagonal line parallel to the seam, and sew along the drawn line. On the sun corner, outside the stitching, trim fabric to a ¼" seam. Make four of these. (ray)

C.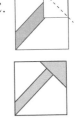

C. Place a sun 2" square on one end of the ray and sew a diagonal seam. Be sure the sun fabric is in the top triangle as shown in the diagram. Make two of these. Make two reversed.

2. Sew the 1" strips together lengthwise. Cut four 2" sections from this set of strips. Assemble according to the piecing diagram.

MINNOW

Cut for one block:

1.	1 minnow	3½" x 5"	rectangle
2.	1 minnow	2" x 3½"	rectangle
3.	6 bckgrnd	2"	square

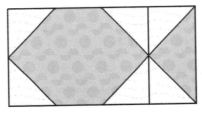

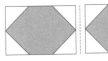

Piecing Diagram

Directions:

1. Place a background 2" square on one corner of a minnow and sew a diagonal seam as shown. Trim outside the stitching to a ¼" seam and press to the triangle. Place a background 2" square on the other end. Sew the opposite diagonal, trim and press.

2. Sew 2" background triangles diagonally on all four corners of the 3½" x 5" minnow rectangle with diagonal seams as shown. Press to the triangles. Assemble according to the piecing diagram.

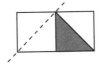

TURTLE

Cut for one block:

1.	1 shell	3½" x 5"	rectangle
2.	2 background	3½"	square
3.	5 turtle, 4 bckgrnd	2" x 3½"	rectangle
4.	6 shell, 10 bckgrnd	2"	square
5.	1 turtle, 2 bckgrnd	1" x 2½"	strip

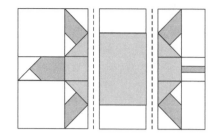

Piecing Diagram

Directions:

1. Make these pieces:

(A) Place a background 2" square on the left end of a 2" x 3½" turtle rectangle and sew a diagonal seam as shown. Outside the stitching, trim fabric to a ¼" seam. Press to the dark. Make three of these. Place a background 2" square on the same end. Sew the opposite diagonal, trim and press. (head)

A.

(B) Take one of (A) and place a background 2" square on the other end. Sew the same diagonal. Make two of these. (C) Make two with the seams sewn to the opposite diagonal.

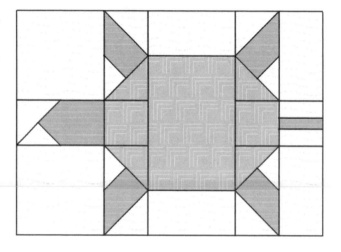

 B. C.

(D) Take (B) and place a shell 2" square on the right end of the pieced rectangle. Sew the opposite diagonal. Trim and press. Make two of these. (legs)

  D.

2. Sew the 1" x 2½" strips together length-wise, with the turtle strip in the middle. Press the seams to one side. Trim to the best 2" section of this set of strips. (tail) Assemble the turtle according to the piecing diagram.

(E) Take (C) and place a shell 2" square on the right end of the pieced rectangle. Sew the opposite diagonal. Trim and press. Make two of these. (legs)

E.

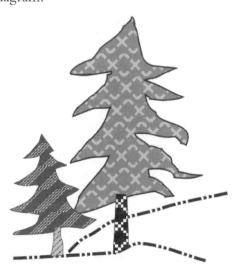

22

FREIGHTER

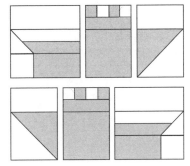

1½" finished square
5" x 11" block with seam allowance

Cut for one block:

1.	1 sky, 1 boat	3⅞"	square
2.	1 boat	3½"	square
3.	1 sky	2" x 5"	rectangle
4.	1 sky, 1 boat	2" x 3½"	rectangle
5.	1 sky, 1 boat	1¼" x 8"	strip
6.	1 boat	1¼" x 3½"	rectangle
7.	2 sky	2"	square

Piecing Diagram

Directions:

1. Cut the sky and boat 3⅞" squares in half diagonally as shown. Sew one of each of the resulting triangles together to make a large half-square. You will have one of each triangle left over.

2. Sew the 1¼" x 8" sky and boat strips together lengthwise. Cut a 5" section and two 1¼" sections from this set of strips.

3. Place a sky 2" square on the left end of the 5" strip section and sew a diagonal seam as shown. Outside the stitching, trim fabric to a ¼" seam. Press to the triangle. Assemble according to the piecing diagram.

1.

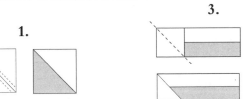

3.

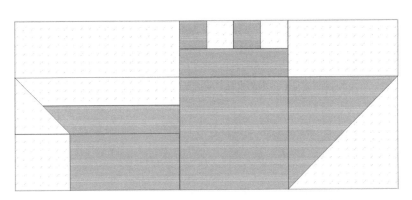

MOON

1½" finished square
6½" x 9½" block with seam allowance

Cut for one block:

1.	2 moon, 2 sky	3⅞"	square
2.	1 moon, 1 sky	3½"	square

Directions:

1. Place the moon and sky 3⅞" squares right sides together. Draw a diagonal line on the back of the lightest fabric. Stitch ¼" away from the line on both sides. Cut on the drawn line to produce two 3½" half-squares. Make two more of these. Assemble according to the piecing diagram.

Piecing Diagram

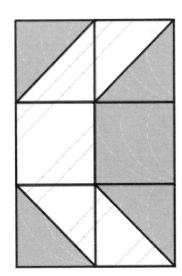

SEAGULL

<table>
<tr><td></td><td></td><td>1½" finished square
20" x 23" block with seam allowance</td></tr>
</table>

Cut for one block:

1.	1 sky	8" x 8"	rectangle
2.	1 sky and 1 piling	6½" x 8"	rectangle
3.	1 sky and 1 wing	5⅜"	square
4.	1 water, 1 wing, 1 sky	5" x 8"	rectangle
5.	1 water	5" x 6½"	rectangle
6.	1 bird	5"	square
7.	1 sky and 1 bird	3⅞"	square
8.	1 sky	3½" x 12½"	rectangle
9.	2 bird	3½" x 8"	rectangle
10.	1 wing	3½"	square
11.	4 sky	2" x 5"	rectangle
12.	1 sky	2" x 3½"	rectangle
13.	1 sky and 1 beak/leg	1¼" x 17"	strip
14.	4 sky, 4 bird, 2 piling	2"	square

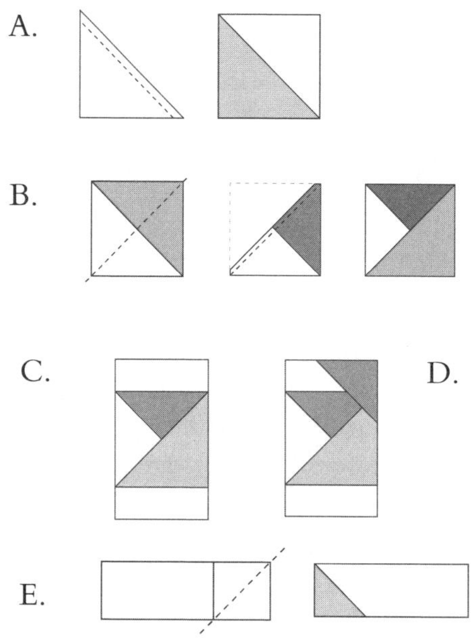

A.

B.

C. D.

E.

Directions:

1. Make these pieces for the tail section:

(A) Cut the sky and wing 5⅜" squares in half diagonally as shown. Sew one of each of the resulting triangles together to make a large half-square. You will have one of each left over.

(B) Draw a diagonal line on the back of the 5" bird square. Place the 5" bird square on the large half-square right sides together and sew the opposite diagonal seam on the drawn line. On one side of the stitching, trim fabric to a ¼" seam as shown in the diagram. Press to the bird triangle. (tail)

(C) Sew a 2" x 5" sky rectangle onto the top and bottom of the tail as shown. (tail section)

(D) Draw a diagonal line on the back of the 3½" wing square. Place the wing 3½" square right sides together on the upper right corner of the tail section and sew diagonally with the drawn line as a guide. Trim and press to the wing triangle.

2. Cut the sky and bird 3⅞" squares in half diagonally as shown. Sew one of each of the resulting triangles together to make a large half-square. You will have one of each left over. (breast)

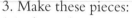

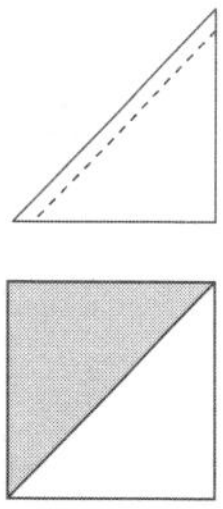

3. Make these pieces:

(E) Place a bird 2" square on one end of a 2" x 5" sky rectangle and sew a diagonal seam as shown. Outside the stitching, trim fabric to a ¼" seam. Press to the triangle. (forehead)

(F) Place a sky 2" square on the bottom left corner of the 3½" x 8" bird rectangle with a diagonal seam as shown. Trim and press to the dark. Make 2 of these. (neck and stomach)

(G) Sew bird 2" squares on the bottom corners, and a sky 2" square on the upper right corner of the 5" x 8" wing rectangle with diagonal seams as shown. Trim and press to the triangles. (wing)

4. Sew the 1¼" sky and beak/leg strips together lengthwise and cut three 5" sections from this set of strips. Then make these pieces:

(H) Place a piling 2" square on the right end of a strip section and sew a diagonal seam as shown. Trim and press.

(I) Place a sky 2" square on the right end of a strip section and sew a diagonal seam as shown. Place a bird 2" square on the left end and sew the opposite diagonal seam. Assemble according to the piecing diagram.

Seagull

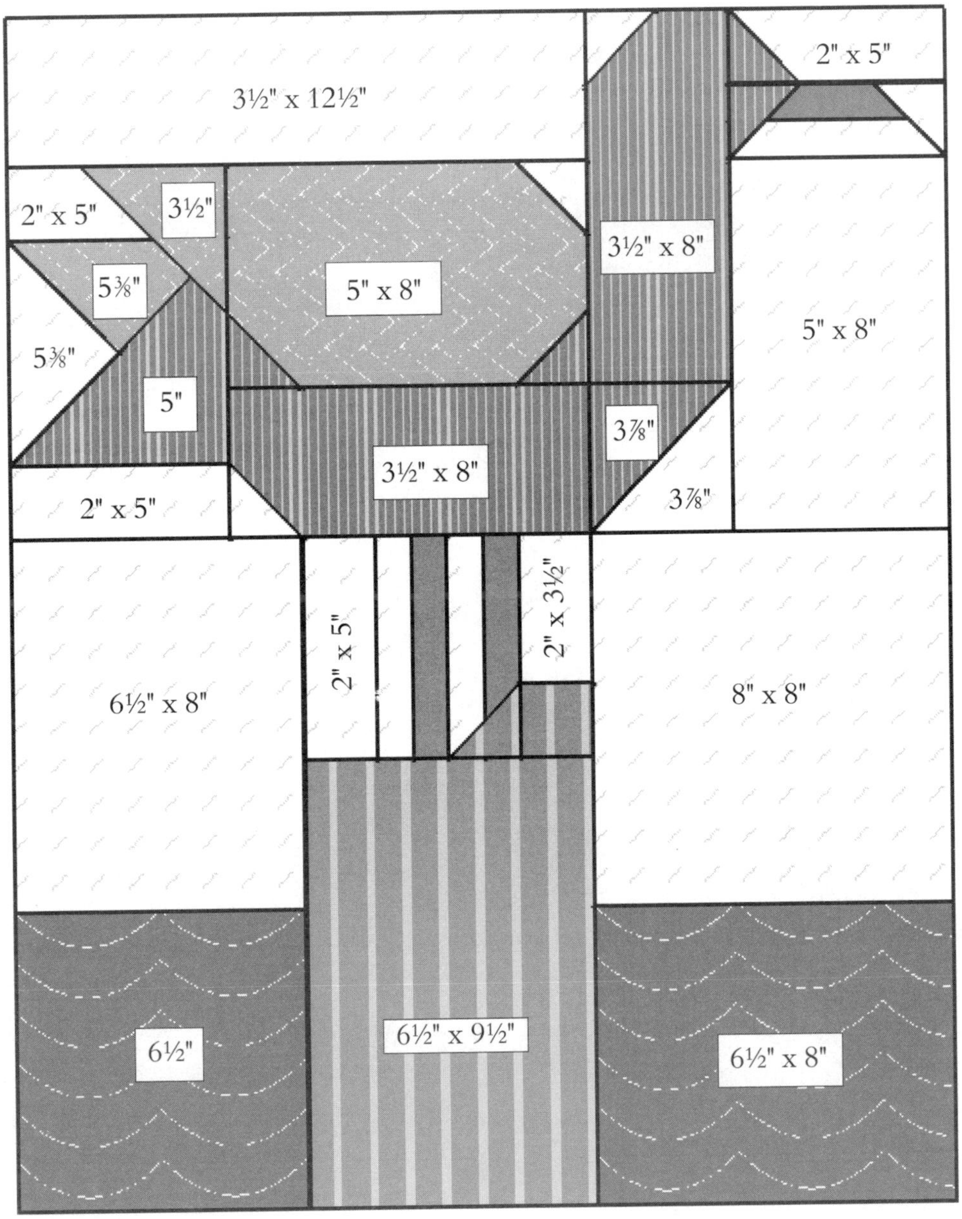

3½" x 12½"
2" x 5"
2" x 5"
3½"
5⅜"
5⅜"
5" x 8"
3½" x 8"
5" x 8"
5"
3½" x 8"
3⅞"
3⅞"
2" x 5"
2" x 5"
2" x 3½"
6½" x 8"
8" x 8"
6½"
6½" x 9½"
6½" x 8"

F.

G.

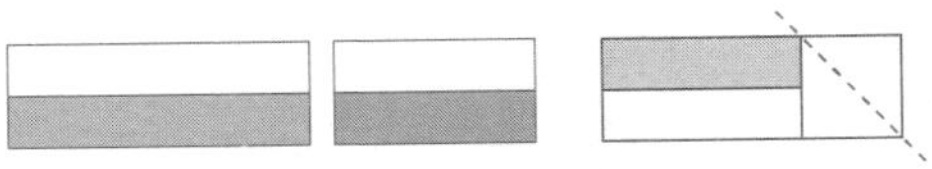

H.

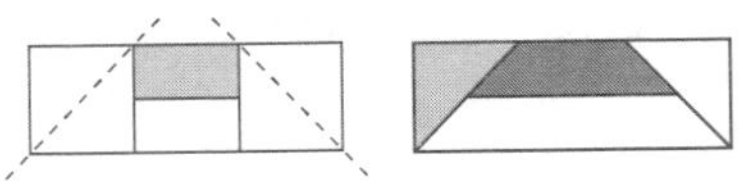

I.

Piecing Diagram

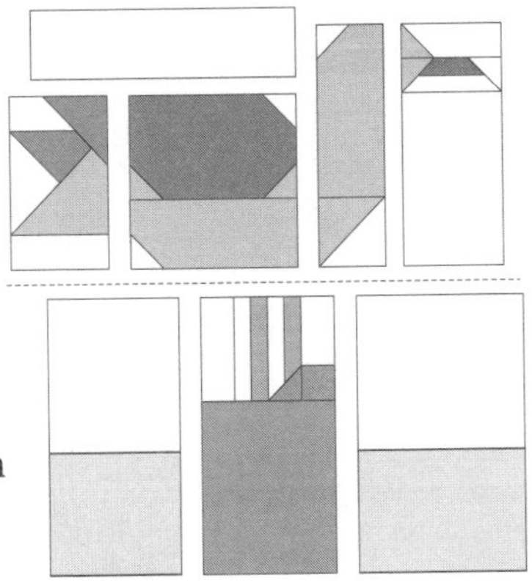

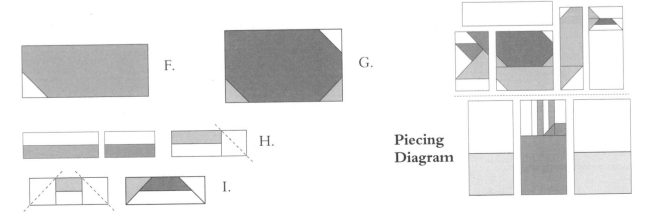

SPORTSCAR

Cut for one block:

1.	1 car	5"	square
2.	1 background	2" x 9½"	rectangle
3.	2 car	2" x 6½"	rectangle
4.	2 background	2" x 5"	rectangle
5.	4 bckgrnd, 1 window, 1 car	2" x 3½"	rectangle
6.	8 background, 4 car, 8 tire	2"	square
7.	2 hubcap, 2 wheelwell	2"	square
8.	1 background, 1 tire	1¼" x 17"	strip
9.	1 bumper color A, 1 bumper color B	1¼" x 6"	strip
10.	2 background	1¼" x 2"	rectangle

4.

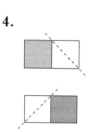

Directions:

1. Sew the tire and background 1¼" x 17" strips together lengthwise. Cut eight 2" sections from this set of strips. (tires) Sew the bumper color 1¼" x 6" strips together lengthwise. Cut two 2¾" sections from this set of strips. (bumpers)

2. Place a tire and a background 2" square right sides together and sew a corner-to-corner diagonal seam. Trim on one side as shown to a quarter inch seam allowance. Press to the dark. This is a 2" half-square. Make 4 of these. Make two car-tire 2" half-squares. Make two wheelwell-tire half-squares.

3. Place a background 2" square on one corner of a car 2" x 6½" rectangle and sew a diagonal seam as shown. Outside the stitching, trim fabric to a ¼" seam. Press to the dark. Make another of these with the seam sewn to the opposite diagonal.

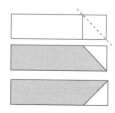

4. Sew a background 2" square diagonally on one end of the 2" x 3½" window rectangle with a diagonal seam as shown. Trim and press to the dark. Sew a background 2" square diagonally on one end of the 2" x 3½" car rectangle with the opposite diagonal seam as shown. Trim and press. Assemble according to the piecing diagram.

Piecing Diagram

Reverse Piecing Diagram

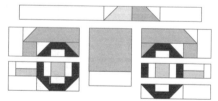

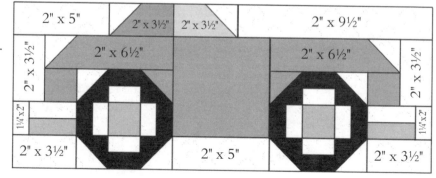

SPORTSCAR FRONT VIEW

1½" finished square
9½" x 12½" block with seam allowance

Cut for one block:

1.	2 background, 1 grill	3½"	square
2.	1 bumper	2" x 11"	rectangle
3.	1 car, 1 background	2" x 6½"	rectangle
4.	1 window	2" x 5"	rectangle
5.	2 car, 2 background	2" x 3½"	rectangle
6.	2 headlight, 2 tire, 6 bckgrnd	2"	square
7.	6 car, 2 background	1¼" x 2"	rectangle

Piecing Diagram

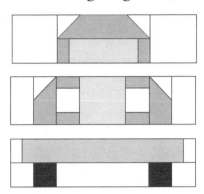

Directions:

1. Place a background 2" square on one end of the car 2" x 6½" rectangle and sew a diagonal seam as shown. Outside the stitching, trim fabric to a ¼" seam. Press to the dark. Place another background 2" square on the other end and sew the opposite diagonal. (roof)

2. Sew a background 2" square on one end of a 2" x 3½" car rectangle with a diagonal seam as shown. Trim and press to the dark. Make another of these with the seam sewn to the opposite diagonal. (fenders)

3. Assemble according to the piecing diagram.

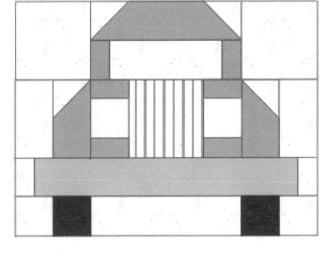

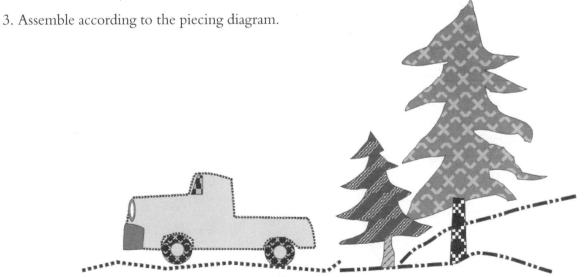

THE MOUNTAIN

Cut for one block:

1.	2 sky, 2 mountain, 1 tree	3⅞"	square
2.	1 sky	3½" x 9½"	rectangle
3.	1 mountain	3½"	square
4.	4 light tree, 2 dark tree	2" x 3½"	rectangle
5.	5 sky, 7 mountain	2"	square

Directions:

1. Make these pieces:

A. Draw a corner to corner diagonal line on the back of the sky 3⅞" square. Place the sky and mountain 3⅞" squares right sides together. Stitch ¼" away from the line on both sides. Cut on the drawn line to produce two 3½" half-square units as shown. You will have one left for another block.

B. Draw a diagonal line on the back of a light tree 3⅞" square. Place right sides together with the remaining mountain 3⅞" square. Stitch as above to produce two 3½" half-square units. You will have one left for another block.

C. Place a half-square unit (B) right sides together with the second sky 3⅞" square. Sew diagonally corner to corner as in diagram. Trim to a ¼" seam.

2. Place a mountain 2" square on one end of a light tree 2" x 3½" rectangle and sew a diagonal seam as shown. Outside the stitching, trim fabric to a ¼" seam. Press to the dark. Place a mountain 2" square on the other end. Sew the opposite diagonal, trim and press. Make 3 of these. Make one with a sky 2" square on the right end. Make two with a dark tree 2" x 3½" rectangles and sky 2" squares.

 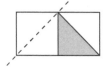

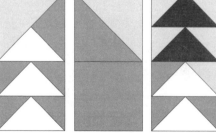

Piecing Diagram

3. Assemble according to the piecing diagram.

28

Tall Ships; 84½" x 107." (left) A breath of the cool sea blows from this elegantly formal quilt by Kathleen Springer. Even a landlubber can imagine filled sails and a fine summers day just by looking at this skillfully colored scene. Flag, mast, and ship are all the same fabric in each ship – a great use of unifying color. Machine quilted by Marianne Roan.

Sailboats and Minnows; 41" x 41." Eda Lee Haas added red ultrasuede flags to the masts of all the little ships and she has added buttons as eyes for the minnows. (Suitable for a wall hanging, but please don't use buttons if you plan to use this as a baby quilt!) Soft colors and lots of precise handquilting add to the depth of detail. Can you see the tiny seagulls stitched into the sky just to the right of each sail? Eda brought out the best in this simple little design.

Angelfish; 81½" x 93½." This quilt had already won two blue ribbons by the time *Quilted Adventures* was published. Eda Lee Haas carefully planned the placement of each color of fish and each ocean fabric, shading from light to dark in the ocean and reversing the shading in the fish. The button eyes add to the impression of glittering water and scales. Eda Lee has named this quilt "Ocean's Bounty." Machine quilted by Debbie Calhoun.

Sports Cars Quilt;
81½" x 92." Fabrics with a
hand-dyed look combine
well with pieces from the
author's stash of Hawaiian
fabrics, garage sale and
thrift-shop finds. The
flickering lights and shad-
ows create an illusion
of mettalic reflections.
The background fabrics
evoke sand, sky, and water.
Would you like to take a
long drive in a fast sports
car? Pieced by Sara
Nephew and machine
quilted by Judy Irish.

Anchors Aweigh; 47" x 53." Scott Hansen
mixed in bits of nautical print fabrics to add
to the reality of this harbor scene. The
vertical row of flags to the left of the tall
ship is communicating real messages. Try
"signal flags" in your Internet search engine
to find out what these messages are. (Of
course, they may conflict. The author
wanted great designs, not to write a letter.)
Machine quilted by Joanne Case.

Riding Bikes; 72½" x 72½." (above) You can ride your bike all day, until the sun goes down and it's time for supper. After supper, you can get on your bike again. Eda Lee Haas used graded shading in every block and setting square of this quilt. Careful planning created a quilt with great visual interest. Silver buttons become the hub for quilted wheel spokes. The patterns in all the background fabrics hint at landscapes, neighborhoods to ride bikes in.

Sports Cars Wallhanging; 44" x 44." (far right) The bond between man and machine is strong. So strong that the author's father named his cars. So it is fitting that cars should decorate our homes. Or maybe it's just fun to have a lap quilt with cars on it. (And a taxi!) Front and side views combine in this small quilt. Results are probably best if colors are not chosen for automotive realism, but rather as artistic decisions. Pieced by Annette Austin and machine quilted by Judy Irish.

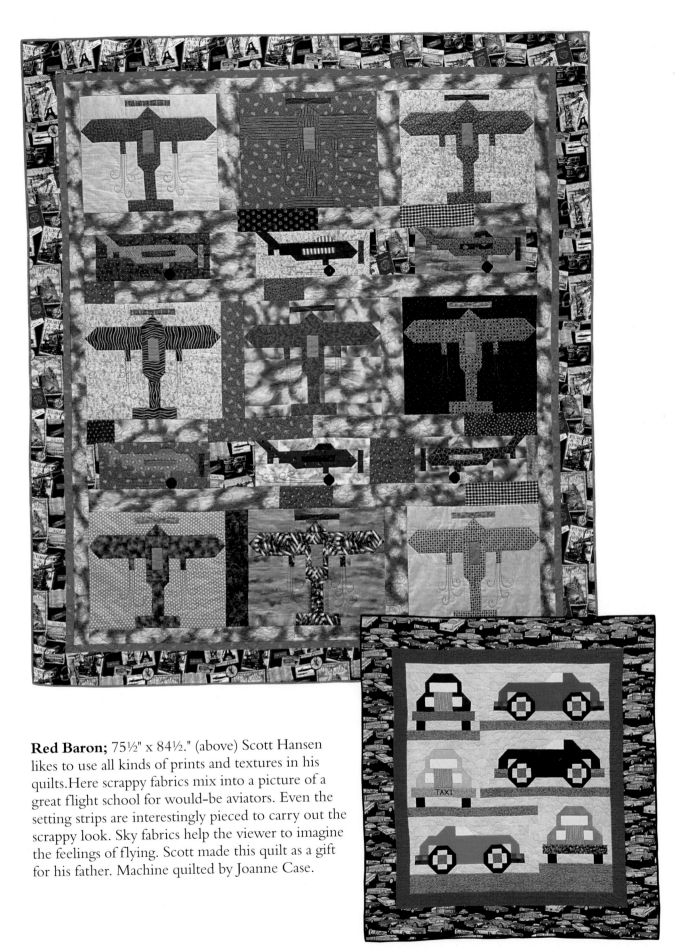

Red Baron; 75½" x 84½." (above) Scott Hansen likes to use all kinds of prints and textures in his quilts.Here scrappy fabrics mix into a picture of a great flight school for would-be aviators. Even the setting strips are interestingly pieced to carry out the scrappy look. Sky fabrics help the viewer to imagine the feelings of flying. Scott made this quilt as a gift for his father. Machine quilted by Joanne Case.

Mariner's Dream;
43" x 43," (upper left)
is more like the author's
dream. Grade school art
class consisted of the
principal giving an
assignment over the loud-
speaker. She lyrically and
hypnotically described
Columbus's ships. The
children had 20 minutes to
draw while classical music
was played. Now I have a
chance to again visit these
white sails in imagination.
Pieced and hand quilted
by Sara Nephew.

Going Places;
60½" x 69½." (left)
Playfulness is the hall-
mark of this twin sized
child's quilt. All the cars,
trains, and trucks look
like toys lined up ready
for fun. Diane enjoyed
choosing her fabrics,
most notably using
printed circles, either
negative or positive, as
tires on some vehicles.
Pieced by Dianne
Coombs and machine
quilted by Judy Irish.

Riverbank; 39½" x 44." (facing page, upper right) Brown and black are colors that a turtle might be. Yet how realistic is a paisly turtle's shell? Aside from that, patterns as beautiful are found in nature. Think of bright green duckweed scattered all over a glossy dark curve, sliding into rippling water. If this quilt evokes natures beauty, it has served its purpose. Pieced and hand quilted by Joan Dawson.

Adventure Sampler; 58½" x 64½." Almost all the blocks in the book made it into this quilt. A grown up might enjoy warming up under this throw while watching TV. But a child could really get into one of the picture blocks while taking a nap or spending a sick day in bed. An action figure could ride a bike, drive a sports car, take a trip in a hot-air balloon. Pieced by Sara Nephew and machine quilted by Judy Irish.

Sea Breeze; 47" x 56."
"Red sky at morning, sailor take warning." And Jean says this is a dawn sky! But for now, all is calm. Hand-dyed fabrics are often ideal for nature-inspired quilts, and they certainly portray sea and sky in this quilt. Pieced and machine quilted by Jean Look-Krischano.

Mountain Air; 59½" x 65½," refreshes the eyes and mind with these cool blues and greens, like our landscapes here in the Pacific Northwest; trees, mountains, and hot-air balloons. The author's oldest granddaughter liked this quilt and wanted to make one immediately for herself. Pieced by Laurie Bevan and machine quilted by Judy Irish.

Hot-Air Balloons;
55½" x 58½." Here's a chance to use your favorite hand-dyed fabrics. They make great sky to mix with these balloons! The pieced blocks vary, some light, some dark, some negative-positive. This adds to the realism of the scene. A balloon festival! Seminole pieced panels are great additions. Pieced by Sara Nephew and machine quilted by Judy Irish.

ADVENTURE QUILTS

SAWTOOTH STAR

Piecing Diagram

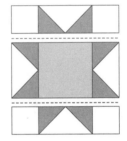

1½" finished square
6½" block with seam allowance

Cut for one block:

1.	1 center square	3½"	square
2.	4 background	2" x 3½"	rectangle
3.	8 dark, 4 bckgrnd	2"	square

Directions:

1. Place a dark 2" square on one end of the background 2" x 3½" rectangle. Sew a diagonal seam as shown. Outside the stitching, trim fabric to a ¼" seam allowance. Press to the triangle. Place another background 2" square on the other end and sew the opposite diagonal. Make four.

2. Assemble according to the piecing diagram.

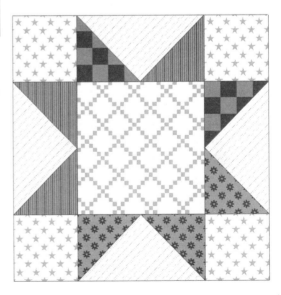

ANGELFISH

Cut for one block:

1.	1 fish, 1 background	3⅞"	square
2.	2 background	3½"	square
3.	5 fish	2"	square

Directions:

1. Place the background and fish 3⅞" squares right sides together. Draw a diagonal line on the back of the lightest fabric. Stitch ¼" away from the line on both sides. Cut on the drawn line to produce two large half-squares.

2. A. Place a fish 2" square on one corner of a 3½" background square and sew a diagonal seam as shown. Outside the stitching, trim fabric to a ¼" seam. Press to the triangle. Sew another fish 2" square on an adjacent corner. Make 2 of these. Take one of (A) and sew a 2" fish square diagonally on another corner as shown.(B) Trim and press to the dark. Assemble according to the piecing diagram.

1.

 A.

 B.

Piecing Diagram **Reverse Piecing**

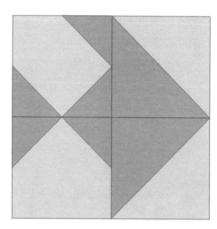

ANGELFISH 2

Cut for one block:

1.	1 fish, 1 bckgrnd	3⅞"	square
2.	1 fish, 3 bckgrnd	2" x 3½"	rectangle
3.	3 fish, 2 bckgrnd	2"	square

Directions:

1. Place the background and fish 3⅞" squares right sides together. Draw a diagonal line on the back of the lightest fabric. Stitch ¼" away from the line on both sides. Cut on the drawn line to produce two large half-squares.

2. Place a fish 2" square on one end of a background 2" x 3½" rectangle and sew a diagonal seam as shown. Outside the stitching, trim fabric to a ¼" seam. Press to the triangle. Make 2 of these. Take one and place another 2" fish square on the other end. Sew the opposite diagonal. Make one of these with reverse values. Assemble according to the piecing diagram.

1.

Piecing Diagram **Reverse Piecing**

 2.

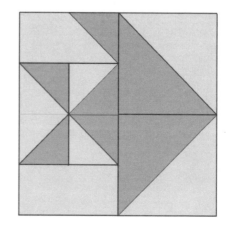

38

SAILBOATS AND MINNOWS

Directions:

1. Piece thirteen Sailboat blocks according to the directions on pg. 17. Piece nine Minnow blocks according to the directions on pg. 21.

1½" finished square
Quilt with borders: 41" x 41"

2. Cut :

12	5"	alternate blocks
4	5"	inner corner squares
9	2" x 3½"	rectangles inner border fabric

All fabric 42" wide prewashed.
Fabric requirements:
¼ yd. sky fabric
⅛ yd. each boat, sail, and water fabric
⅓ yd. alternate square, inner border fabric
⅓ yd. minnow fabric
½ yd. minnow background fabric
⅓ yd. inner border fabric
¼ yd. each inner, outer corner squares
¾ yd. outer border fabric

3. Assemble the Sailboat blocks and alternate blocks into rows and sew the rows together according to the diagram. Sew a 2" x 3½" rectangle of inner border fabric to the tail of each minnow and sew the minnows into four borders of three blocks each. Add a 2" x 32" strip of inner border fabric to the bottom of each border section as shown in the quilt diagram. Sew the left and right borders on. Add the 5" inner corner squares on both ends of the remaining two borders. Sew the top and bottom Minnow borders on the quilt.

4. Cut four 5" outer border squares and four 5" x 32" outer borders. Sew on the left and right outer borders. Add the 5" corner squares to both ends of the remaining two borders and sew them on top and bottom to complete the quilt.

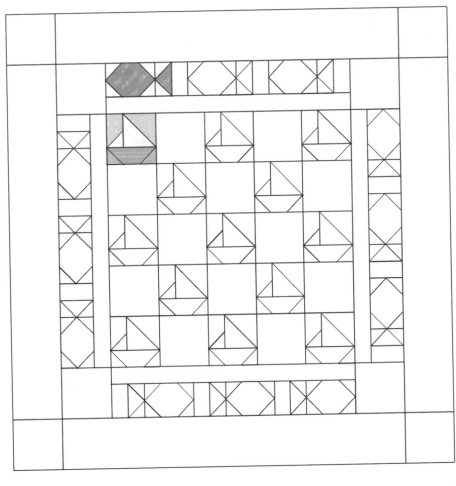

RIDING BIKES

Directions:

1. Piece eight Bicyclist blocks and eight reverse blocks according to the directions on pg. 10.

2. Cut:

9	3½"	corner squares
24	3½" x 12½"	setting strips

Assemble the quilt top according to the diagram. Add a 3½" inner border and a final 5" outer border to complete the quilt.

All fabric 42" wide prewashed.

Fabric requirements:

2" strip each of face fabric and foot fabric
¼ yd. pants fabric
⅓ yd. each shirt fabric and road fabric
¾ yd. bike fabric
2 yds. background fabric
⅛ yd. corner square fabric
1½ yds. setting strip fabric
1¼ yds. inner border fabric
1½ yds. outer border fabric

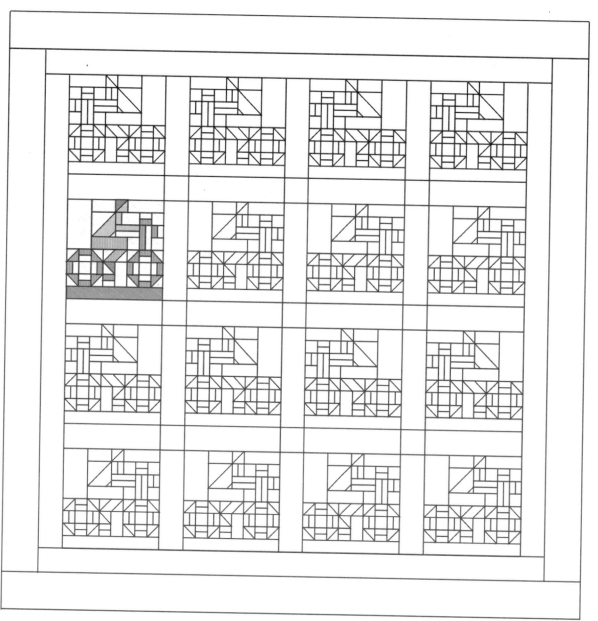

ANGELFISH

1½" finished square
Quilt with borders: 81½" x 93½"

Directions:

1. Piece blocks according to the directions on pg. 38.
42 Angelfish block, 32 Angelfish block reversed
6 Angelfish 2 block, 4 Angelfish **2** block reversed

2. Cut 84 6½" squares for alternate blocks. According to the quilt diagram: Make two-row sets of blocks and alternate squares. Make four sets and three sets reversed. Sew the sets together. Add a 5" border to complete the quilt.

All fabric 42" wide prewashed.

Fabric requirements:
3¾ yds. each fish fabric and background fabric
2¾ yds. alternate square fabric
1½ yds. border fabric

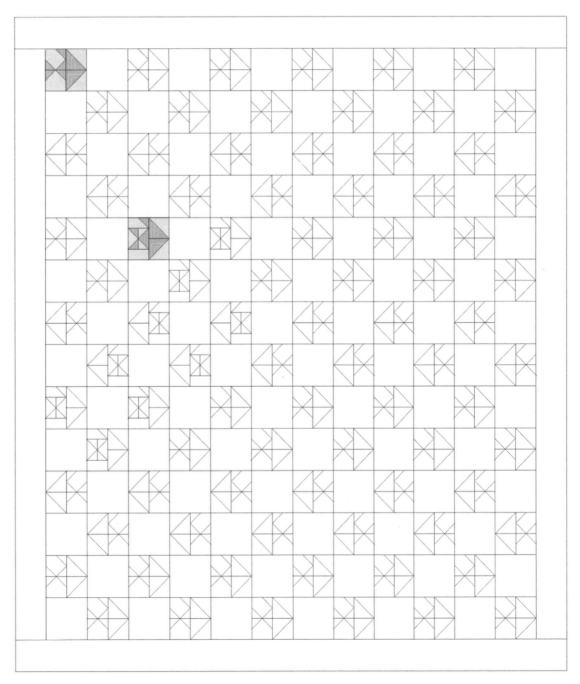

41

RIVERBANK

1½" finished square
Quilt with borders: 39½" x 44"

Directions:

1. Piece six Turtle blocks according to the directions on pg. 22. (You may wish to make a tail strip set 13" long and cut six 2" sections.)

2. Cut for setting strips:

3	3½" x 8"	vertical setting strips
2	3½" x 24½"	horizontal setting strips

3. Assemble according to the quilt diagram. Add a 2" inner border. Cut for the Seaweed borders (see pg. 17):

82	background	2" x 3½"	rectangle
86	seaweed	2"	square
4	background	2"	square

All fabric 42" wide prewashed.
Fabric requirements:
¼ yd. each turtle head and shell fabric
½ yd. each turtle and seaweed background fabric
⅓ yd. seaweed fabric
½ yd. each setting strip and outer border fabric

Assemble the top and bottom Seaweed borders as shown in the quilt diagram. Sew onto the quilt. Assemble the left and right Seaweed borders as shown and sew on. Add a final 5" border to complete the quilt.

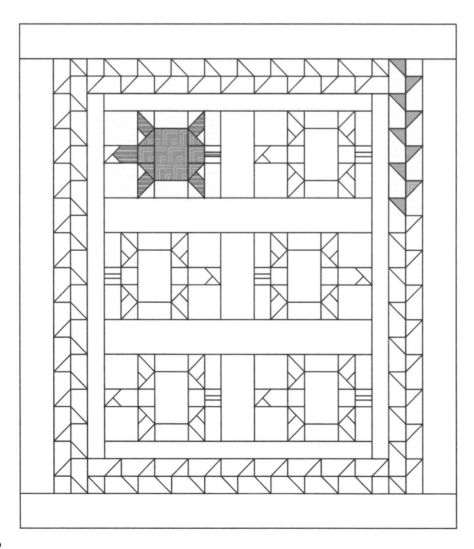

MARINER'S DREAM

All fabric 42" wide prewashed.

Fabric requirements:

Use scraps and fat quarters, or use ⅓ yd. each
light/dark sky fabric
¼ yd. sail fabric
2" square flag fabric
2" strip water fabric
4" strip sun fabric, moon fabric
⅛ yd. boat fabric
⅓ yd. inner border fabric
½ yd. outer border fabric

Directions:

1. Piece the blocks listed below in quantities given:

1 Moon pg. 23	1 Tall Ship pg. 18
1 Sun pg. 21	5 Sawtooth Star pg. 37
5 Sawtooth Star, reverse values	

2. Cut one 2" x 18½" rectangle of water fabric. Make 12 additional water/sky 2" half-squares according to the directions on pg. 19. Add these to the bottom of the Tall Ship block as in the quilt diagram.

3. Cut from sky fabric and sew in the position indicated:

| 1 | 2" x 8" | top of Sun block |
| 1 | 5" x 9½" | left of Moon block |

Sew together and add to top of Tall Ship block according to the quilt diagram. Sew a row of five Sawtooth Star blocks to the left and right of the ship section. Add a 2½" inner border and a final 5" outer border to complete the wall hanging.

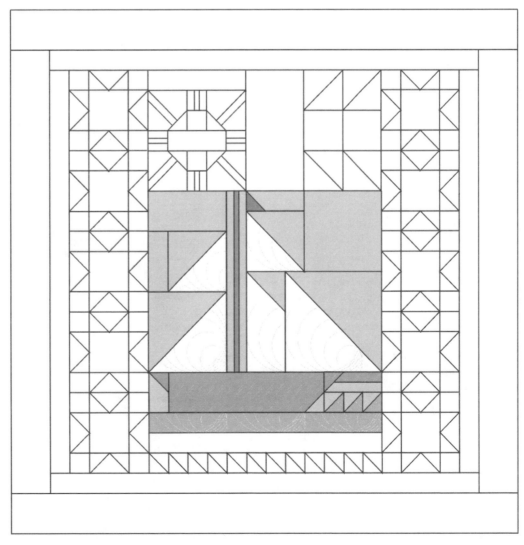

TALL SHIPS

1½" finished square
Quilt with borders: 84½" x 107"

All fabric 42" wide prewashed.

Fabric requirements:

2¼ yds. sky fabric

1¼ yds. sail fabric

¾ yd. each water and boat fabric

¼ yd. mast fabric

2" strip flag fabric

½ yd. corner square fabric

2½ yds. setting strip fabric

1¾ yds. border fabric

Directions:

1. Piece 12 Tall Ship blocks according to the directions on pg. 18.

2. Cut setting strips and corner squares according to the directions below:

20	5"	corner squares
31	5" x 18½"	setting strips

3. According to the quilt diagram: Sew four rows of 3 Tall Ship blocks and 4 vertical setting strips, beginning and ending with setting strips. Sew five rows of 4 corner squares and 3 horizontal setting strips, beginning and ending with corner squares. Sew the rows together in order. Add a 6½" outer border to complete the quilt.

Sea Breeze

1½" finished square
Quilt with borders: 47" x 56"

Directions:

1. Piece the blocks below according to the directions given:

Seagull pg. 24   Sailboat pg. 17

2. Cut one of each fill-in piece for placement as listed below:

water	5" x 6½"	under Sailboat
sky	6½" x 21½"	over Sailboat
sky	8" x 20"	over Seagull
sky	2" x 5"	right of Sailboat

All fabric 42" wide prewashed.

Fabric requirements:
¼ yd. each bird and wing fabric
1¼" strip beak/leg fabric
¼ yd. piling fabric
¾ yd. sky fabric
¼ yd. water fabric
4" x 6" sail fabric
2" x 6" boat fabric
½ yd. inner border fabric
¾ yd. outer border fabric

3. According to the quilt diagram: Sew the 2" x 5" rectangle to the right of the Sailboat, and the water piece below. Add the correct sky pieces above both blocks. Sew the resulting two sections together to make the quilt top. Add a 3½" inner border and a final 5" outer border to complete the quilt.

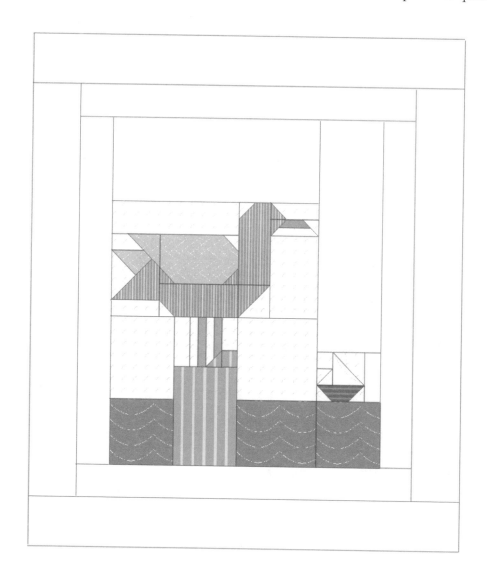

HOT-AIR BALLOONS

Directions:

1. Piece 15 Hot-Air Balloon blocks according to the directions on pg. 12.

2. Cut twenty 6½" x 9½" rectangles of sky fabric. According to the diagram, make rows of blocks and sky rectangles and sew the rows together.

3. Add a 2" inner border and a final 5½" outer border to complete the quilt.

1½" finished square
Quilt with borders: 55½" x 58½"

All fabric 42" wide prewashed.
Fabric requirements: *(lots of fat quarters)*
1 yd. total balloon fabrics (3⅛" strip each 2 balloons)
1½ yd. total sky fabrics
2" strip basket fabric
1¼" strips mixed bright colors for Seminole patterns
⅓ yd. inner border fabric, ¾ yd. outer border fabric

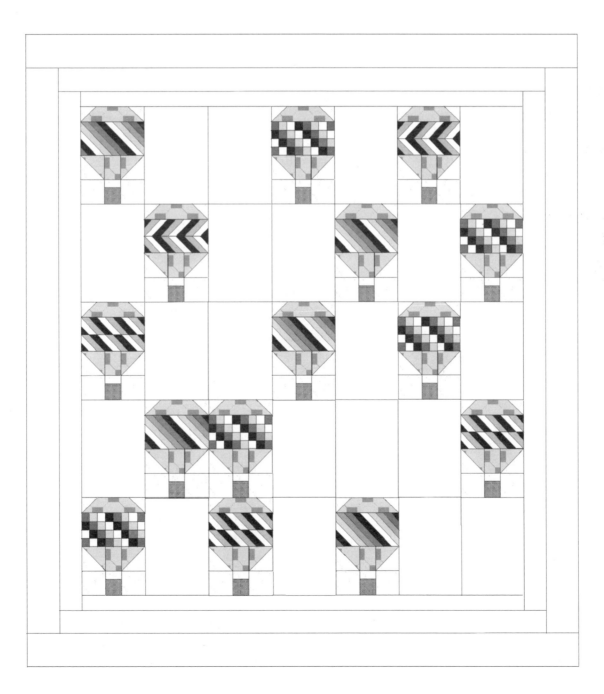

GOING PLACES

1½" finished square
Quilt with borders: 60½" x 69½"

Directions:
1. Piece blocks in the quantities listed below:
1 Hot-Air Balloon, pg. 12
2 Jet, pg. 4
1 Helicopter, pg.6
1 School Bus, pg. 5
1 Sedan, pg. 7
1 Pickup and 2 Pickup Reversed, pg.7
1 Little Van, pg.6
1 Big Van, pg.5
1 Truck, pg. 4
1 Locomotive, pg. 8
1 Coal Car, pg. 8
1 Freight Car, pg. 3
1 Coach Car, pg. 9
1 Caboose, pg. 9
2 Freighter pg. 23
2 Sailboat pg. 17

All fabric 42" wide prewashed.
Fabric requirements:
2" strip each of car, pickup, jet, window, tire, door, water, and boat fabric (use scraps and strips for doors, windows, wheels, balloon, basket, etc.)
¼ yd. each road, and truck fabric
⅛ yd. each school bus, freighter, train car, locomotive, and sail fabric
⅔ yd. long setting strip fabric, sky fabric, bckgrnd fabric
¾ yd. inner border fabric
1 yd. border fabric

2. Cut for small setting strips and sew where indicated:

1.	1 sky fabric	2" x 9½"	left of balloon
2.	4 sky fabric	5" x 9½"	right of balloon, right of top jet, top of one jet, bottom of other jet
3.	4 background	2" x 8"	top of pickup 3x, top of little van
4.	4 background	2" x 9½"	top of big van, top of sedan
5.	6 background	3½" x 6½"	between all vehicles
6.	1 background	2" x 32"	top of train cars (not Locomotive)
7.	5 sky	3½" x 5"	between boats plus extra one on right
8.	2 background	2" x 6½"	both sides of train

3. Cut for roads:

　　1¼" strip of road fabric

　　1¼" strip of yellow

　　2" strip of road fabric

Sew together lengthwise in order. Make two of these. Measure the rows of blocks and cut the roads to match the average measurement. (Should be 45½".) Sew the roads below the two automotive rows.

4. Cut for rails:

　　1¼" strip of ground fabric

　　1¼" strip of railroad ties

Sew together lengthwise. Then cut 2" sections from this set of strips. You will need 30 of these.(Or use a 2" strip of striped fabric cut across the stripe.)Sew a 1¼" strip of rail on either side of the railroad ties. Then sew these tracks below the train.

5. Assemble rows as shown in the quilt diagram. Cut four 3½" long horizontal setting strips to the same measurement as the rows of blocks, (should be 45½") and sew together alternately with the rows as shown in the quilt diagram. Add a 3½" inner border and a final 5" border to complete the quilt.

GOING PLACES

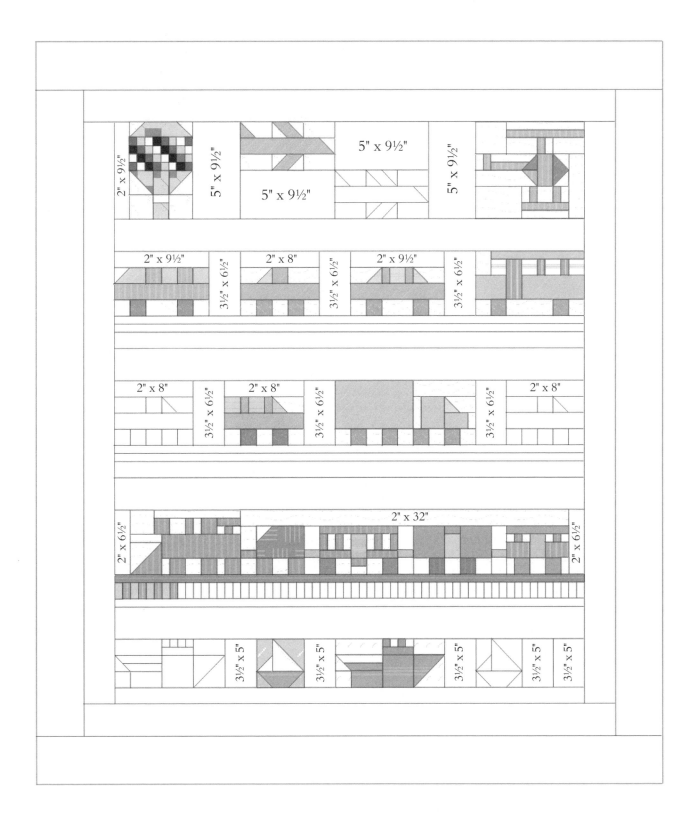

LET'S GO! BABY QUILT

No Photo Given

Directions:

1. Piece blocks in the quantities listed below:
1 Hot-Air Balloon, pg. 12
1 Jet pg. 4
1 Helicopter, pg. 6
1 Pickup, pg.7
1 School Bus, pg. 5
1 Big Van, pg. 5
1 Locomotive, pg. 8
1 Coal Car, pg. 8
1 Freight Car, pg. 3
1 Caboose, pg. 9
1 Freighter pg. 23
2 Sailboat pg. 17

1½" finished square
Quilt with borders: 47" x 51½"

All fabric 42" wide prewashed.
Fabric requirements:
2" strip each of car, pickup, jet, window, tire, door, water, and boat fabric (use scraps for most vehicles, basket, and other details)
¼ yd. each sky and road fabric
⅛ yd. each school bus, freighter, train car, rail, locomotive, and sail fabric
⅔ yd. long setting strip fabric
1 yd. border fabric

2. Cut short setting strips:

A.	2 sky fabric	2" x 9½"	left of balloon, top of big van
B.	3 sky fabric	5" x 9½"	right and left of jet, under jet
C.	4 background	2" x 6½"	left and right of train row, left and right of cars row
D.	2 background	3½" x 6½"	both sides of school bus
E.	5 sky fabric	3½" x 5"	both sides of sailboats and left of freighter
F.	1 sky fabric	2" x 5"	left end of sailboat row

3. **Cut for road:**
> 1¼" strip of road fabric
> 1¼" strip of yellow
> 2" strip of road fabric

Sew together lengthwise in order. Measure the row of blocks and cut the roads to match the average measurement. (should be 38") Sew the road below the automotive row.

4. **Cut for rails:**
> 1¼" strip of ground fabric
> 1¼" strip of railroad ties

Sew together lengthwise. Then cut 2" sections from this set of strips. You will need 30 of these. (Or use a 2" strip of striped fabric cut ACROSS the stripe.) Sew a 1¼" strip of rail on either side of the railroad ties. Then sew these tracks below the train.

5. Assemble four rows as shown in the quilt diagram. Cut three 3½" horizontal setting strips to the same measurement as the rows, and sew together alternately with the rows of blocks as in the quilt diagram. Add a final 5" border to complete the quilt.

LET'S GO! BABY QUILT

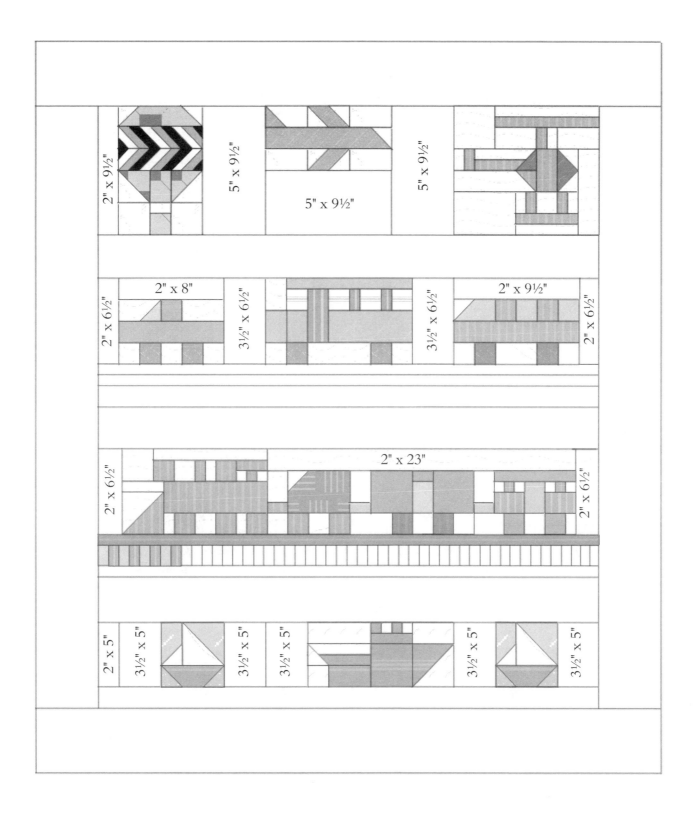

RED BARON

Directions:

1. Piece nine Topplane blocks according to the directions on pg. 14. Piece six Sideplane blocks according to the directions on pg. 15.

2. Cut setting strips and fill-in pieces according to the directions below. Use scraps or fat quarters to get a nice mix of dark, light, or aeronautical fabrics.

1.	4	6½"	Sideplane setting squares
2.	4	2" x 6½"	Sideplane setting strips
3.	6	3½" x 15½"	Topplane setting strips
4.	4	3½" x 60½"	Horizontal setting strips

3. Sew the Sideplane blocks into two horizontal rows of three, alternating with the 6½" setting squares. Finish the ends of the rows with the Sideplane 2" x 6½" setting strips. Sew the Topplane blocks into three horizontal rows of three, alternating with the Topplane 3½" x 15½" setting strips.

4. Sew the rows and horizontal setting strips together as shown in the quilt diagram. Add a 3½" inner border and a final 5" border to complete the quilt.

All fabric 42" wide prewashed.

Fabric requirements:

1½ yds. sky fabric

1 yd. plane fabric (OR: if you use a different color for the wing in the TOPPLANE blocks, add ¼ yd. to wing fabric and use ¾ yd. plane fabric)

1¼" selvage to selvage strip wing fabric

2" strip each cockpit and tire fabric

1⅓ yds. setting strips and squares

1 yd. inner border

1¼ yds. outer border

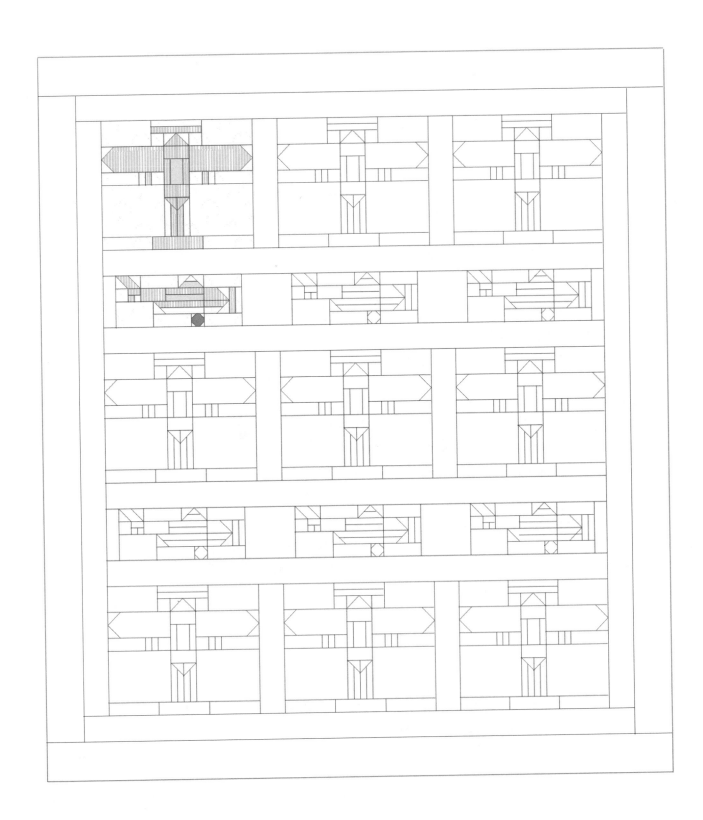

Sports Cars Wallhanging

1½" finished square
Quilt with borders: 46" x 47½"

All fabric 42" wide prewashed.
Fabric requirements:
2" strip each hubcap, headlight, window fabric
2" strip each bumper, wheelwell, front view car fabric
3½" strip grille fabric
⅛ yd. tire fabric
¼ yd. each side view car fabric
¾ yd. block background fabric
⅓ yd. each road and sky setting strip fabric
(or can use other colors)
½ yd. inner border fabric
¾ yd. border fabric

Directions:

1. Piece one Sportscar block and two reversed Sportscar blocks according to the directions on pg. 26. Piece three Sportscar Front View blocks according to the directions on pg. 27.

2. Cut setting strips according to the dimensions on the quilt diagram below. (You may wish to measure sections and adjust setting strips to match.) Use scraps or fat quarters if desired. Sew the sections together as shown to make the quilt top. Add an inner 2¾" border and a final 5½" border to complete the quilt.

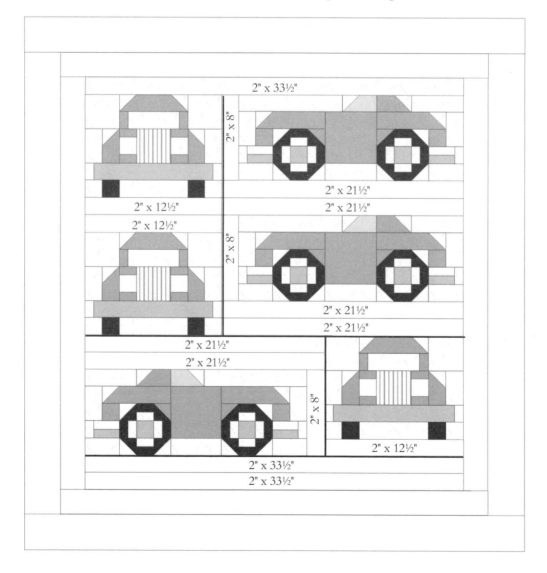

MOUNTAIN AIR

Directions:

1. Piece eight Mountain blocks according to the directions on pg. 28. Piece eight Hot-Air Balloon blocks according to the directions on pg. 12 (using two of each Seminole pattern).

2. Cut from setting strip fabric:

12	3½" x 9½"	vertical setting strips
3	3½" x 39½"	horizontal setting strips

Assemble according to the quilt diagram. Add a 3½" inner border.

3. Cut 34 each light and dark 3⅞" squares Pieced Border fabric. Draw a corner-to-corner diagonal line on the back of the light squares. Place the light and dark 3⅞" squares right sides together. Stitch ¼" away from the line on both sides. Cut on the drawn line to produce two 3½" half-squares (or use another quick method to produce these half-squares). Make 68 half squares altogether.

4. Make four rows of seventeen 3⅞" half-squares. Sew a Pieced Border row on right and left, then sew one on top and bottom. Add a final 3½" border to complete the quilt.

All fabric 42" wide prewashed.

Fabric requirements:

⅓ yd. balloon fabric, balloon block sky fabric
2" strip basket fabric, dark tree fabric
¼ yd. mountain block sky fabric, light tree fabric
½ yd. mountain fabric
⅔ yd. cloud fabric (above the mountain)
1¼" strips of bright solids for Seminole piecing (at least 5 colors)
½ yd. setting strip fabric
1 yd. inner border fabric
½ yd. each pieced border fabric (2 colors)
1¼ yds. outer border fabric

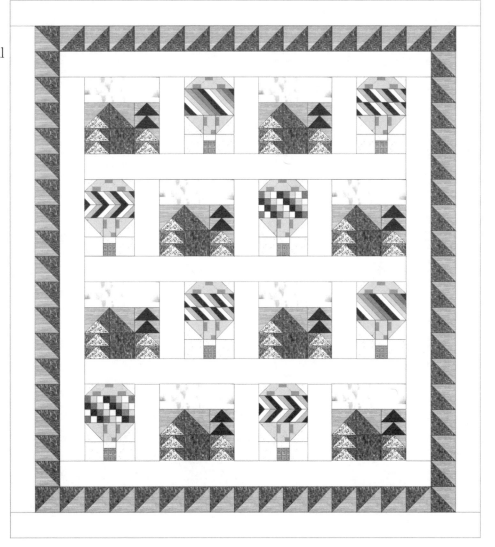

ANCHORS AWEIGH

All fabric 42" wide prewashed.

Fabric requirements:

¾ yd. sky fabric

⅓ yd. sail fabric

⅛ yd. ship and freighter fabric

2" strip water fabric

2" strip each red, white, yellow, black flag fabric

⅛ yd. blue flag fabric

4" flag setting strip fabric

½ yd. each anchor and anchor background fabric

¼ yd. ships panel setting strip fabric

¼ yd. narrow inner border fabric

¼ yd. seaweed fabric

½ yd. seaweed background fabric (if different color)

¾ yd. wide inner border fabric (4¾")

¾ yd. outer border fabric (3½")

1½" finished square

Quilt with borders: 47" x 53"

Directions:

1. Piece the blocks below according to the directions on the pages indicated:

1	Tall Ship, pg. 18
1	each Freighter, Reverse Freighter, pg. 23
1	each Sailboat, Reverse Sailboat, pg. 17

2. Cut:

2	2" x 18½"	boat setting strip
2	3½" x 5"	boat setting rectangle

Assemble into a boat section as shown in the quilt diagram.

3. Make one of each Nautical Flag Block according to the directions on pg. 18. Then cut:

6	2" x 6½"	horizontal setting strip
7	2" x 3½"	vertical setting strip

Place a 2" x 3½" setting strip on the right end of each flag. Then assemble all the flag blocks into a vertical panel, alternating the 2" x 6½" setting strips with the flag blocks as shown. Sew the flag section onto the left of the boat panel. Add a 1¼" narrow border around this center section.

4. *These borders are directional so be sure to follow the quilt diagram.* Make two Seaweed Borders each eight basic units long plus one 2" square or half-square according to the directions on pg. 17. Cut two wide inner borders 4¾" x 24½" and sew onto the top or bottom of the Seaweed Border as shown. Sew these pieced borders above and below the center quilt panel from #3 above. *You may wish to assemble the Anchor-Seaweed borders in #6 below, measure their length, and then adjust the 4¾" width of the wide inner border as necessary.*

5. Make two Seaweed Borders ten basic units long according to the directions on pg. 17. Cut two wide inner borders 4¾" x 30½". Sew onto the left or right of the Seaweed Border as shown. *These borders are directional so be sure to follow the quilt diagram.*

6. Make four Anchor blocks, according to the directions on pg. 16. Sew top and bottom to the left and right pieced Seaweed Border from #5 above. Sew these Anchor-Seaweed borders left and right onto the quilt top. Add a final 3½" border to complete the quilt.

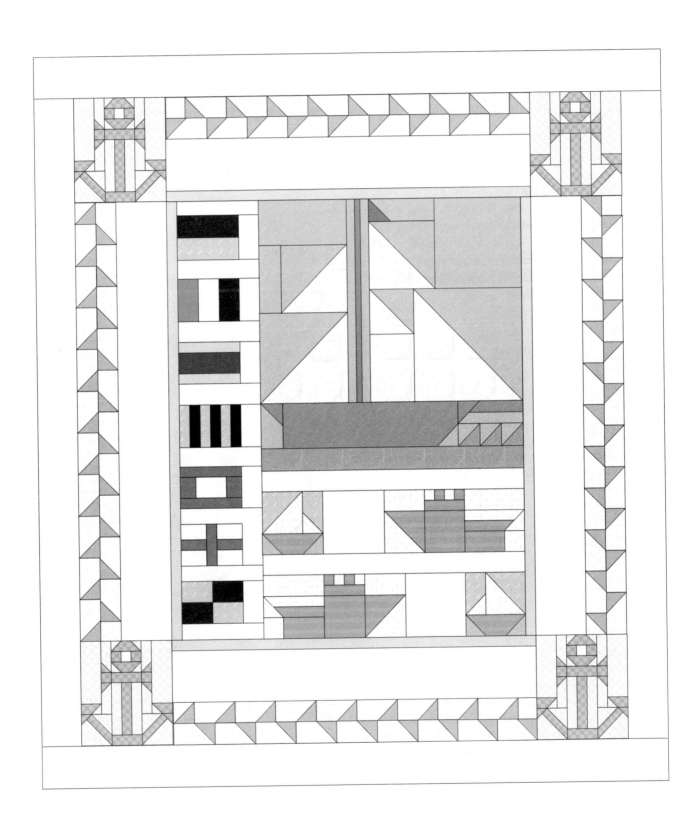

SPORTS CARS QUILT

1½" finished square
Quilt with borders: 87½" x 93½"

All fabric 42" wide prewashed.

Fabric requirements:
⅛ yd. window fabric (scraps and strips)
scraps and strips of bumper fabrics
⅓ yd. each of five different car fabrics
½ yd. each of two additional car fabrics
⅔ yd. yellow fabric
2 yd. black fabric
⅔ yd. each two sky fabrics
2 yds. background fabric
1 yd. inner border fabric
1¼ yds. outer border fabric

Directions:

1. Piece seven Sportscar blocks and seven Sportscar blocks reversed according to the directions on pg. 26. *For the tires, you may wish to use a method to produce half-squares in quantity. See pgs. 10-11.* Piece seven sky sections made from two different 4¼" x 20" pieces of sky fabric. Sew the Sportscar blocks and the sky sections into seven rows, alternating these blocks with 4¼" x 8" setting strips. Follow the quilt diagram when assembling the rows. (Cars can point in either direction.)

2. Cut:

1.	road	1¼"	strip
2.	yellow	1¼"	strip
3.	road	2"	strip
4.	car	2"	strip

Sew strips 1, 2, and three together lengthwise in order. (Measure the rows of cars, average, and piece the length of this setting strip to match. Mine was 67".) Then sew this setting strip on under each row of cars with the narrowest strips under the tires as shown. Sew on a strip of car color after you have all the rows laid out, to help choose the best color. Sew the rows and setting strips together to make the quilt top. Add a 3½" inner border and a final 4½" border to complete the quilt.

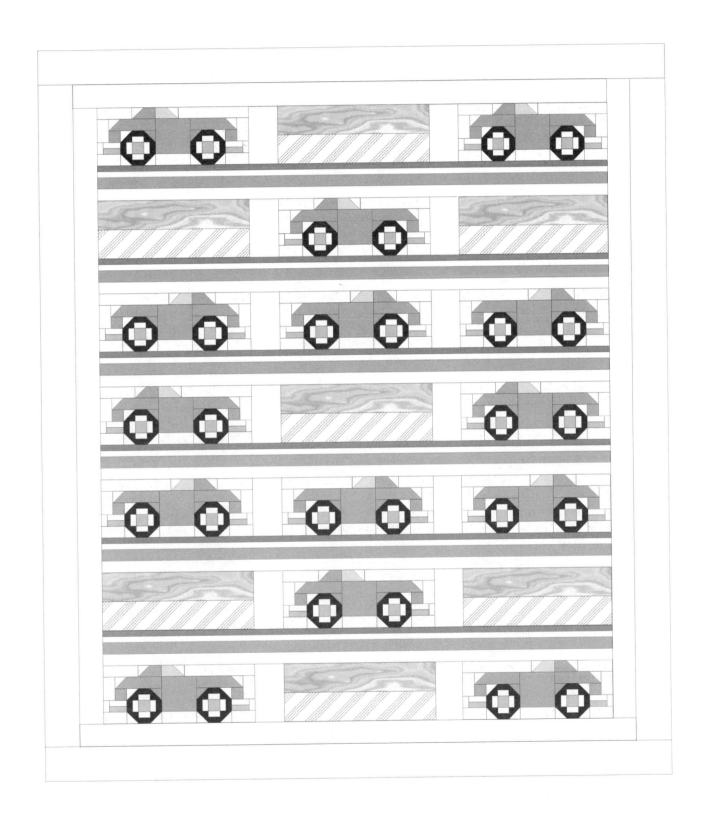

ADVENTURE SAMPLER

All fabric 42" wide prewashed.
Fabric requirements:
various scraps of fabric, enough for each block
4" strip of road fabric (setting strips)
½ yd. sky fabric (setting strips and fill-in pieces)
½ yd. additional setting strip fabric (various strips and scraps)
½ yd. inner border
1 yd. border fabric

Directions:
1. Piece one of each block below according to the directions on the pages given. Then make two of Sawtooth Star on pg. 42.

Jet pg. 4	School Bus pg. 5
Helicopter pg. 6	The Mountain pg. 28
Bicyclist pg. 10	Hot-Air Balloon pg. 12
Topplane pg. 14	Tall Ship pg. 18
Turtle pg. 22	Moon pg. 23
Freighter pg. 23	Sportscar pg. 26
Sportscar Front View pg. 27	
Angelfish pg. 38	

2. Cut one of each fill-in piece according to the directions below. Use scraps or fat quarters to get a nice mix of dark, light, or medium fabrics.

A.	3½" x 6½"	under Hot-Air Balloon
B.	3½" x 6½"	above School Bus
C.	3½" x 8"	left of Angelfish
D.	3½" x 11¾"	under Helicopter
E.	3½" x 12½"	left of Sawtooth Stars
F.	4¼" x 5"	right of Freighter
G.	4¼" x 6½"	left of Jet
H.	5¾" x 6½"	right of Jet
I.	7¼" x 8"	right of Sportscar
J.	8" x 9½"	right of Sportscar Front V.

> 1½" finished square
> **Quilt with borders: 58½" x 64½"**

3. Cut one of each setting strip according to the directions below.

K.	2" x 6½"	right of School Bus
L.	2" x 9½"	below Angelfish
M.	2" x 9½"	below Turtle
N.	2" x 11"	left of Turtle
O.	2" x 14"	above Jet
P.	2" x 15¼"	above Freighter
Q.	2" x 18½"	above **and below** Topplane
R.	2" x 20" (road)	under Sportscar Front V.
S.	2" x 20" (sky)	above Sportscar
T.	2" x 27¼" (road)	below Sportscar
U.	2¾" x 9½"	left of Helicopter
V.	2¾" x 24½"	left of Tall Ship

4. Sew the resulting three sections (as shown in the quilt diagram) together to make the quilt top. Add a 2" inner border and a final 5½" border to complete the quilt.

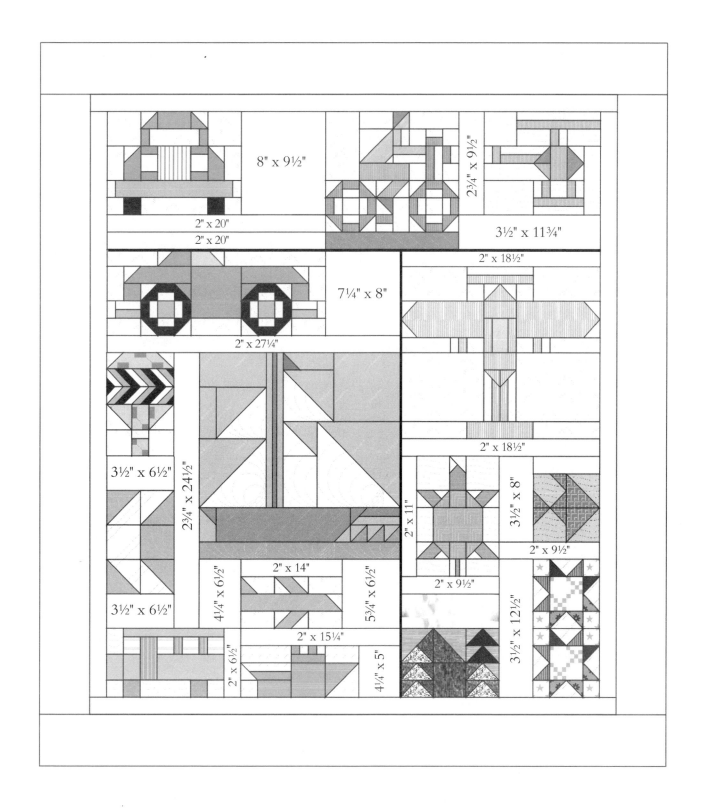

CUTTING AND PIECING

General Directions - *Tools*

You may already have most of the tools needed to piece the quilts in this book. But they will be listed and discussed one by one below so that everything necessary is ready when you begin to make your blocks.

The **rotary cutter** is what makes these patterns quick. Choose the brand and size that is comfortable for you to use and learn how to assemble and clean it. The author prefers a middle-sized Olfa® cutter. After using your rotary cutter carefully for a while, you will no longer dull the blade with little nicks from running over pins, etc.

ROTARY CUTTER

You will need a **cutting mat** that will keep the rotary blade sharp and protect your table or counter top. Mats come in various colors, with or without rulings on both sides. Choose a color that is easy for you to look at. Rulings are great, but at first you may wish to check the measurements of cut pieces, as the rulings on mats are sometimes not accurate.

Mats come in many sizes, too. One of the larger sizes is good for protecting a table at home, but a smaller size works better for carrying to class. (Don't leave a cutting mat in a car on a warm day.) Eventually a well-used mat will need to be replaced. But first try turning it over and wearing out the back of the mat also.

Be sure to cut at a table or counter that's the right height for you!

Easy Cutting and Piecing

There are many **rulers** that work with rotary cutters. My favorite is are the 6" x 12" by Omnigrid®. Other sizes are often convenient to cut smaller pieces. The 6" square is a nice size to work with.

After all the pieces are cut, you will need a sewing machine that takes a nice straight stitch, perhaps a press cloth, and an iron and ironing board.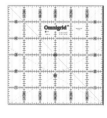

Strips, Squares, and Rectangles

Cut a strip first, then cut the strip into all the shapes you need. Begin by pressing prewashed fabric selvage to selvage. Then bring the fold to the selvages and press again. Use a 6" x 12" ruler to cut a strip the desired width. The short cut needed (12" rather than 24") helps keep the ruler and the rotary cutter under your control.

Use the top ruler edge, bottom ruler edge, or a measuring line across the ruler or on the cutting board to keep the fabric straight.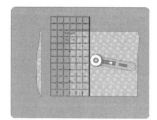

Trim edge straight, then cut the strip.

> TIP: If you do get a strip that's a little zigzag, you can still cut some pieces from it (but not at the places where the strip is not straight).

Get the Most From Your Fabric

First cut a strip to match the narrowest measure of the biggest piece. Then look for other pieces of the same fabric that share this width and cut them next.

Example: The largest piece needed is a 6½" square. So you cut a 6½" strip and cut the squares. Further down the list you see a piece from the same fabric that measures 2½" x 6½". So you can cut 2½" pieces from the same width.

Then trim the strip to the next width needed, and cut as many pieces from that width as possible. Often you'll be able to get all the pieces needed out of the first strip you cut.

> Tip: Also look for pieces where two will fit into the width. Say you had a strip width of 4½", and needed some pieces 2" x 6½". You could cut a piece 4½" x 6½", trim to 4", and get two of the smaller pieces from it. Generally cut all the largest pieces first, before trimming any width from the strip.

Shape Recognition

You will gradually begin to recognize the various sizes and shapes that you are cutting, and be able to pick them up as needed. But don't hesitate to check measurements with a ruler before sewing one piece on to another. As always, use a ¼" seam for piecing. No small triangles are used when piecing these blocks. Instead, squares are used, and sewn diagonally onto square corners of other squares or rectangles.

> TIP: To prevent confusion when cutting pieces for a complex pattern, stack all pieces of the same size and pin them together. Write the size on a Post-It® note and stick it on top.

The Most Important Seam

This fast piecing often requires the quilter to sew a diagonal seam across a small square. You can learn to eyeball the correct seam line, or try one of the tips below:

> TIP: Draw a diagonal line on the back of the fabric square with pencil, chalk, or a wash-out marker.
> OR: Fold and crease the square from corner to corner to make a sewing line.
> OR: Use a ruler to draw a line with a permanent fine-tip marker (ink does wear off after a while) on your sewing machine in front of the needle. The line should be perpendicular to the straight front edge of the sewing machine. Keep diagonal corners of the square on the drawn line.

Large Half-Squares

A half-square is a square divided in half diagonally (two triangles sewn together). Usually one half is dark and the other half is light. Big triangles are relatively simple to work with. They are obtained by cutting a square in half diagonally using a ruler and rotary cutter.

This triangle is then sewn to a triangle of another color, to get a large half-square. This requires sewing two bias edges together. Handle your fabric lightly as you are sewing the triangles together. Many sewing machines sew well straight ahead. Lay the two triangles right sides together and gently bring them under the presser foot with the minimum guidance required, allowing the machine to do the work.

Practice makes it easier. Even if the seam gets a little stretched in sewing, pressing with a steam iron or wet press cloth generally will correct any distortion.

Small Half-Squares

In this book, small half-squares are produced by placing two squares right sides together and sewing diagonally. The fabrics then are trimmed to a ¼" seam on one side of the stitching. If you need a lot of small half-squares made from the same fabrics, use one of the fast methods for which there are papers or templates.

> TIP: If you need two large half-squares in the same fabrics, don't cut the light and dark squares in half. Instead, lay the light and dark squares right sides together, draw a diagonal line on the back of the light fabric square with pencil or a wash-out marker, and sew a ¼" seam each side of this line. Cut along the pencil line for two pre-sewn large half-squares.

> TIP: The rule is usually to press to the dark. Occasionally bulky seams make it easier to press to the light.

Chain Sewing

I used to have a sewing machine that cut the top thread with each stitch unless there was fabric under the presser foot. So I learned to chain sew. Pieces to be sewn are fed under the needle with minimum space between, and cut apart later. This speeds up the sewing and prevents the messiness of long tails of thread draped everywhere, needing to be trimmed. Many quilters keep a piece of scrap fabric to use at the start and end of each chain.

Pressing Techniques

Try a wet press cloth as an alternative to the steam iron. Use a dry iron for most of the pressing. This avoids the weight of the iron causing sore elbows and arms during extended piecing sessions. Then when one block or unit is complete, take a piece of old sheet (my favorite, but muslin works too), dampen it in a sink, wring it out, and lay it flat over the pieced block, with the block right side up. Run the hot iron lightly over the damp cloth to dampen the block underneath. Then lay the wet press cloth aside, and dry and flatten the block with the hot iron. Turn the block over afterwards to check that the seams are all laying correctly. You can tug at the block a bit as you press it to square it up. This is like blocking a sweater. Block your block.

Special Thanks To These Manufacturers

Sara Nephew

Sara Nephew graduated from Alverno College in Milwaukee, WI, with an art major. She was trained as a jeweler, and showed her cloisonne' enamel work in national shows. She began her first quilt in 1967, using corduroy squares from her daughter's rompers. In the 80's she began to apply her art training seriously to quilting and in 1984 started a business making and repairing quilts.

She has since originated a series of tools for rotary cutting isometric shapes, authored 17 books, and become an internationally known teacher and lecturer. Sara now lives in Clearview, WA, with her husband, Dale. She is enjoying her three grown children and her four grandchildren. Dale is retired, and he helps in the business.

Other Products From Clearview Triangle

New Series - Quick Picture Quilts

HH-17	9.95	Book - Happy Halloween
TX-24	9.95	Book - Town & Country

60° Triangle Books and Tools

B-25	19.95	Book - Big Book Of Building Block Quilts
B-21	14.95	Book - Sensational 6-Pointed Star Quilts
B-10	14.95	Book - Building Block Quilts
SR-20	16.95	Super 60 (Combination Triangle Tool)
DG-27	6.75	Diamond Guide (Super 60 Add-On)
MP-3	11.50	8" Mini-Pro
M-15	11.50	Metric Triangle
SR-26	16.95	Metric Super 60
CT-1	8.00	6" triangle
CT-2	15.00	12" triangle
GP-12	5.95	2-sided Graph Paper-Pad of 30 sheets

Bargain Corner

ZO-18	15.00	Book - Patchwork Zoo
EA-7	5.00	Book - Easy & Elegant Quilts
MA-14	5.00	Book - Mock Appliqué
MC-16	4.00	Book - Merry Christmas
TX-23	4.00	Book - Special Times
NL-19	3.00	Book - New Labels
PR-22	3.00	Pattern-Pigma® Pen Roll-Up

Order Subtotal	Shipping
$0.00-5.99	$1.99
6.00-10.99	$2.99
11.00-20.99	$3.99
21.00-30.99	$4.99
31.00-40.99	$5.99
41.00-65.99	$6.99
66.00-100.99	$7.99
101.00 +	$9.00

Wash. residents add 8.6% sales tax
We take Visa and Mastercard.

CLEARVIEW TRIANGLE
8311 - 180th St S. E.
Snohomish, WA
98296-4802 USA
Tel: 1-360-668-4151
Fax: 1-360-668-6338
Orders: 1-888-901-4151

E-mail: ClearviewT@cs.com
Website: www.clearviewtriangle.com